201 Dynamite Job Search Letters

By Ron and Caryl Krannich

CAREER AND BUSINESS BOOKS AND SOFTWARE

101 Dynamite Answers to Interview Questions
101 Secrets of Highly Effective Speakers
201 Dynamite Job Search Letters
America's Top 100 Jobs for People Without a Four-Year Degree
America's Top Jobs for People Re-Entering the Workforce
America's Top Internet Job Sites
Best Jobs for the 21st Century
Change Your Job, Change Your Life
The Complete Guide to Public Employment
The Directory of Federal Jobs and Employers
Discover the Best Jobs for You!
Dynamite Cover Letters
Dynamite Resumes
Dynamite Salary Negotiations
Dynamite Tele-Search
The Educator's Guide to Alternative Jobs and Careers
Find a Federal Job Fast!
From Air Force Blue to Corporate Gray
From Army Green to Corporate Gray
From Navy Blue to Corporate Gray
Get a Raise in 7 Days
High Impact Resumes and Letters
I Want to Do Something Else, But I'm Not Sure What It Is
Interview for Success
The Job Hunting Guide: Transitioning From College to Career
Job Hunting Tips for People With Not-So-Hot Backgrounds
Job Interview Tips for People With Not-So-Hot Backgrounds
Job-Power Source and Ultimate Job Source (software)
Jobs and Careers With Nonprofit Organizations
Military Resumes and Cover Letters
Moving Out of Education
Moving Out of Government
Nail the Job Interview!
No One Will Hire Me!
Re-Careering in Turbulent Times
Savvy Interviewing
Savvy Networker
Savvy Resume Writer

TRAVEL AND INTERNATIONAL BOOKS

Best Resumes and CVs for International Jobs
The Complete Guide to International Jobs and Careers
The Directory of Websites for International Jobs
International Jobs Directory
Jobs for Travel Lovers
Mayors and Managers in Thailand
Politics of Family Planning Policy in Thailand
Shopping and Traveling in Exotic Asia
Shopping in Exotic Places
Shopping the Exotic South Pacific
Travel Planning On the Internet
Treasures and Pleasures of Australia
Treasures and Pleasures of Bermuda
Treasures and Pleasures of China
Treasures and Pleasures of Egypt
Treasures and Pleasures of Hong Kong
Treasures and Pleasures of India
Treasures and Pleasures of Indonesia
Treasures and Pleasures of Italy
Treasures and Pleasures of Mexico
Treasures and Pleasures of Paris and the French Riviera
Treasures and Pleasures of Rio and São Paulo
Treasures and Pleasures of Santa Fe, Taos, and Albuquerque
Treasures and Pleasures of Singapore and Bali
Treasures and Pleasures of Singapore and Malaysia
Treasures and Pleasures of South America
Treasures and Pleasures of Southern Africa
Treasures and Pleasures of Thailand and Myanmar
Treasures and Pleasures of Turkey
Treasures and Pleasures of Vietnam and Cambodia

201 Dynamite
Job Search Letters

Writing Right for Today's New Job Market

Fifth Edition

Ronald L. Krannich, Ph.D.
Caryl Rae Krannich, Ph.D.

IMPACT PUBLICATIONS
Manassas Park, VA

Fifth Edition

Library of Congress Cataloguing-in-Publication Data

Krannich, Ronald L.
    201 dynamite job search letters: writing right for today's new job
  market /Ronald L. Krannich, Caryl Rae Krannich. – 5th ed.
      p. cm.
  Includes bibliographical references and index
    ISBN 1-57023-232-6 (alk. paper)
    1. Résumés (Employment) 2. Job hunting. I. Title: Two hundred one
  dynamite job search letters. II. Krannich, Caryl Rae. III. Title.
  HF5383.K714   2004
  808'.06665 – dc21   2004112725

Publisher: For information on Impact Publications, including current and forthcoming publications, authors, press kits, online bookstore, and submission requirements, visit Impact's website: www.impactpublications.com.

Publicity/Rights: For information on publicity, author interviews, and subsidiary rights, contact the Media Relations Department: Tel. 703-361-7300, Fax 703-335-9486, or e-mail: info@impactpublications.com.

Sales/Distribution: All bookstore sales are handled through Impact's trade distributor: National Book Network, 15200 NBN Way, Blue Ridge Summit, PA 17214, Tel. 1-800-462-6420. All other sales and distribution inquiries should be directed to the publisher: Sales Department, IMPACT PUBLICATIONS, 9104 Manassas Drive, Suite N, Manassas Park, VA 20111-5211, Tel. 703-361-7300, Fax 703-335-9486, or e-mail: info@impactpublications.com.

Contents

Directory of Featured Job Search Letters

Cover Letters for Different Situations 156-167

Resume Letters As Job Applications 170-188

Follow-Up Letters That Get Action 191-214

Thank You Letters 216-248

Preface

FINDING A JOB IS ALL ABOUT clearly communicating your qualifications and goals to potential employers. You do this through numerous mediums and channels, from letters and resumes to the mail, faxes, e-mail, telephone, and face-to-face interviews. Your ultimate goal is to get a job interview that hopefully turns into a job offer and a job you both do well and enjoy doing – one that leads to a rewarding career.

But communicating your qualifications to potential employers is easier said than done. After all, you are often dealing with strangers who know little or nothing about you as either a person or a professional. Furthermore, most people are not used to writing resumes and letters, nor initiating contacts with strangers. If you are like many other job seekers, you would rather be doing something else with your time than trying to get employers to take notice of your qualifications and invite you to interviews.

Like giving a speech before a group, writing letters to strangers is a task many people prefer avoiding. It's more than just work. For some, it's filled with anxiety. For others, it's simply difficult to do – they don't know what to say or how to say it. After all, they may make foolish and embarrassing mistakes.

But write these letters you must! In 25 years of working with numerous job seekers, we've noticed one important self-defeating behavioral pattern that relates to the art of writing: most job seekers lack goals, focus, and persistence. Indeed, their resumes are often helter-skelter collections of names, dates, activities, and wishful hype with little evidence of individual career goals or patterns of performance. They engage in time-honored writing rituals without a clear understanding of how their written words can produce results. Indeed, many job seekers often wander aimlessly in a sea of job possibilities, hoping that their timing and luck will connect them to a great new job. Not knowing what they want to do, they often present a confusing picture to employers who need to predict a candidate's future performance. Instead, employers must constantly **interpret** what really lies behind the letters and resumes they receive from unfocused job seekers.

When done properly, letter writing forces job seekers to organize their thoughts, clarify goals, and give their job search direction. As you will see in the many examples outlined in this book, powerful job search letters can bring coherence and direction to a job search. In the hands of a persistent, determined, and well-focused job seeker, these letters produce the desired results – invitations to job interviews and eventual job offers.

This book is designed to take the anxiety out of writing job search letters. It assumes a certain level of focus (you should have a clear idea of what you want to do) and persistence (follow up, follow up, follow up) on your part. If use judiciously, it should result in moving your job search into the direction of more job interviews and offers.

> *When done properly, letter writing forces job seekers to organize their thoughts, clarify goals, and give their job search direction.*

The 201 job search letters presented in the following pages are written for a variety of job search situations. Taken together, they represent an important compendium of job search communication. They review important strategies and approaches for handling various stages of the job search. Examined individually, they are addressed to specific situations requiring some form of written communication. Each letter is structured around two key job search considerations:

- the job search process – from skills identification to conducting research, networking, interviewing, and accepting an offer.

- principles of effective job search communication and writing.

Career counselors will find many of these letters fit perfectly into their job search and career planning approaches. Job seekers will find these examples answer many of their questions concerning *"what to do," "what to say," "how to say it,"* and *"what to do next."* In contrast to other books on job search letters, this one pulls together a large variety of job search communications that represent important actions you should take at various stages of your job search. As such, it is more than just another job search letter example book. It represents particular communication strategies for conducting an effective job search. For example, in the following pages you will find letters to:

- start, as well as stop, your job search
- develop contacts and uncover job leads
- broadcast your qualifications to potential employers
- follow up on earlier communication
- develop good relations with a new employer

You will see how important it is to clearly communicate your purpose, energy, enthusiasm, intelligence, and likability in these letters – important qualities sought by employers in job interviews but which are difficult to express in the format of a resume. You will notice how job seekers approach the networking process – one of the most important yet least understood job search approaches. You will learn that the simple social grace of writing a brief thank you letter can make a real difference in how you are perceived by an employer, regardless of the quality of your cover letter and resume. You will learn why many letters must include a follow-up statement – a critical element missing in most examples of job search letters.

Except in the face-to-face interview, there is no better way of expressing your purpose, energy, enthusiasm, intelligence, and likability than in the form of job search letters.

Overall, our examples represent the richness and texture – as well as the complexities, challenges, and frustrations – found in most job searches. What emerges from these letters are some of the basic realities involved in finding a job. As such, these letters lay bare some of the most important communication that takes place at every stage of an effective job search.

Whatever you do, make sure your job search letters represent the **unique you**. The temptation, of course, is to creatively plagiarize others' examples rather than produce your own job search letters from scratch. We strongly recommend that you avoid the pitfalls of simply copying someone else's letter – no matter how good. For how you write your letters and express your own interests, personality, and drive will say a lot about how you will handle yourself on the job. Creatively plagiarizing letters produced by others may indicate how you plan to do the job – cutting corners rather than fully using your abilities and skills. Use our letters as departure points for identifying the types of letters you need to write and what you need to include in your letters, especially the importance of follow-up statements and expressions of purpose, energy, enthusiasm, intelligence, and likability – qualities employers want to hire in addition to your experience and qualifications. Except in the face-to-face interview, there is no better way of expressing these qualities than in the form of job search letters.

Please be forewarned that the names and addresses in our examples are fictitious. If you attempt to send letters to these names and addresses, your mail will most likely be returned with the appropriate notation – "Address Unknown."

This new edition again includes one of the most powerful, and usually overlooked, job search letters you can write – "T" letters. We outline the importance of these letters on page 93 as well as offer examples on pages 133 and 148. If you respond to classified ads and vacancy announcements, be sure to do so with this type of letter. Like the resume letters in Chapter 8, "T" letters can easily substitute for resumes. Best of all, they often produce phenomenal results – very high response rates from employers who immediately invite writers of these letters to job interviews. We also include a directory of all 201 job search letters ("Directory of Featured Job Search Letters") on pages iv-viii. It again includes a separate chapter (Chapter 12) on planning and evaluation, including a self-evaluation instrument so you can quickly assess the quality of each letter you produce and distribute. We've also included planning forms that will help you produce a large variety and volume of letters to accelerate your job search. This chapter is designed to help you effectively implement a job search plan in which letter writing plays a key role in generating interviews and job offers. A Career Resource section at the end of the book (pages 270-271) includes several additional job search resources available through Impact Publications and its online resource center – www.impactpublications.com.

We wish you well in your job search. Finding a job is often a tough and frustrating road to travel. But with the help of our numerous examples of effective job search communication, you should be able to give your job search renewed direction as you clearly communicate your technical or professional qualifications, as well as other personal and professional qualities, to employers. In the end, you should get positive results if you avoid the pitfalls and follow the basic principles outlined in Chapters 2 and 12 as well as expressed in the 201 dynamite job search letter examples presented in Chapters 3-11.

Ron and Caryl Krannich

krannich@impactpublications.com

201 Dynamite Job Search Letters

1

Write Your Way to a Great New Job

ETTER WRITING IS ONE of the most neglected and abused job search skills. Preoccupied with writing and perfecting resumes, most job seekers overlook one of the most important activities for getting a job interview or offer – writing job search letters. Or they only focus on writing a cover letter to accompany their resume. Worse still, they casually compose cryptic e-mail messages that tend to showcase their incompetence!

But one of the best kept secrets of getting job interviews and offers is the role of several types of job search letters. Expertly crafted and linked to your major strengths, these letters are often more effective than a resume. They also serve as important extensions to job interviews. If you want to conduct a dynamic job search, make sure you write a variety of powerful job search letters throughout all phases of your job search, including the day you are hired!

A Stranger's Best Friend

You are what you write. At least in the eyes of potential employers – to whom you are probably a stranger – how you initially present yourself in writing says a great deal about your fitness for future employment. How you write and distribute your written messages – be it by mail, fax, or e-mail – says something very important about you, your capabilities, and your potential value to others. What you say and how you say it provide clues to your patterns of behavior and future performance.

If you neglect your writing skills, make common writing and distribution errors, or fail to follow up your written communications, you will diminish your value in today's highly competitive job market. This should not happen to you. Indeed, as you will quickly discover in the chapters that follow, our 52 communication principles and 201 dynamite letter examples should help you better develop your own powerful letters for achieving job and career success.

Become More Effective

Are you an effective writer who can persuade others to take actions that benefit you? Can you write letters that will have an important impact on your career? Do you regularly write letters that command the attention of employers who call you for job interviews? Do you routinely send thank you letters to individuals who assisted you or invited you to interviews? Are you a thoughtful person who makes a habit of communicating your personal and professional values to others in writing? Is the content of your letters employer-centered rather than self-centered? Do you mention **benefits to others** rather than benefits to yourself? Do you know how to use e-mail and faxes to best communicate your qualifications to employers? Do you always communicate your "best self" to others in writing?

If you answer "no" or "maybe" to any of these questions, then this book is for you. In the following pages, we'll show you how to **get results** from a wide variety of letters that are central to conducting an effective job search.

Write It Right

Most job hunters have a very simple view of what they need to do in order to find a job – primarily write resumes and conduct job interviews. Many even put the job-finding process on autopilot by submitting electronic versions of their resume to searchable online databases and then wait to be contacted by employers who discover their qualifications online. Few see letter writing as important to their job search. Yet, it is increasingly clear that the letter writing process, involving the creation of several types of job search letters, plays a critical role in conducting an effective job search. In fact, many employers report that a thoughtful job search letter sometimes is more important to offering the job than the resume or interview.

Individuals who write powerful letters also are those who tend to write excellent resumes and conduct effective job interviews. They have a clear understanding of the role letter writing plays in the overall job search process. They view letter writing as an essential ingredient in their efforts to persuade others to do things they ordinarily would not do – invite them to an interview as well as offer them the job. Going beyond just writing attractive letters, they produce excellent form and content that clearly communicate their qualifications to potential employers. Furthermore, understanding today's fast-paced and increasingly electronic world of communications, these individuals are savvy at mailing, faxing, and e-mailing their letters to the right people; they especially know how to use e-mail in their job search. Above all, they know how to write, produce, distribute, and follow up their letters with maximum impact.

> _Employers increasingly report that a thoughtful job search letter is sometimes more important to offering a job than the resume or interview._

That is our task in the following pages – to make sure you have the tools to become an effective job seeker who can write right and thus write your way to job search success. We'll outline key letter writing, production, distribution, and follow-up principles as well as provide you with 201 examples of letters to be used for numerous job search occasions. These examples illustrate the key principles in writing right for job search success.

Job Search Letters That Get Results

A **dynamite job search letter** is any letter designed to promote the process of finding a job and thereby enhancing your career visibility and acceptance to others. An effective job search letter gets read and responded to in positive ways. Such letters grab the attention of readers who take the following actions:

1. Remember you.
2. Refer you to others.
3. Contact you for further information.
4. Invite you to a job interview.
5. Offer you a job.

As illustrated in the chart on page 4, job search letters encompass more than just cover letters. They include several additional job search situations that go beyond the submission of resumes accompanied by cover letters.

Normally written during each phase of the job search, these letters are key building blocks for conducting an effective job search campaign. These letters also should be written while on the job. They not only help you find a job, they may help you keep your job and develop long-term professional and personal relations. Such letters contribute to shaping your network of relationships.

Major Types of Job Search Letters

Phase	Process	Types of Letters
1	Assess abilities, skills, & interests.	Inquiry for assessment services.
2	State an objective.	None.
3	Conduct research.	Information-gathering letters on organizations, employers, and employment services. Approach letters to individuals.
4	Write resume and letters.	Cover letters, resume letters, and "T" letters.
5	Network for information, advice, and referrals.	Approach, thank you, and follow-up letters.
6	Conduct job interviews.	Thank you and follow-up letters.
7	Negotiate the job offer.	Thank you letter.

Job search letters may become the most important and powerful letters you will ever write. Their central purpose is to get others to take actions they might not normally take had you not written the letter. Above all, you want your letter recipients to promote your career goals. These letters also have several other purposes:

- **Gather information for your reference and decision-making.** During each stage of your job search, you need important information for making additional decisions. Above all, you need to learn about the shape and direction of the job market. You should know about specific jobs that interest you. You want to gather as much information as possible about specific employers and their organizations. You do this by using the Internet, making telephone calls, meeting with individuals, and writing letters for information.

- **Communicate your major qualifications and strengths to employers.** These letters come in three major forms: cover letters, resume letters, and "T" letters. A **cover letter** always accompanies a resume. It should grab the attention of the reader who, in turn, reviews the resume in depth. A **resume letter** substitutes for a resume. It is written when it is more appropriate to summarize your qualifications in the format of a letter rather than submit a resume. Resume letters provide individuals with flexibility in targeting their qualifications to different employers. A "T" letter is a very targeted letter that summarizes one's qualifications in direct reference to an employer's stated needs.

- **Make important contacts for developing a critical network of job search relationships.** Networking plays a central role in communicating your goals and marketing your qualifications to others. And letters play a central role in building your network. These letters have two purposes. First, you want to write several letters informing family members, friends, professional acquaintances, and other contacts about your decision to seek new employment. Second, you want them to take action by requesting they refer you to others who might be able to give you additional information, advice, and referrals. You will want to write other letters to strangers in anticipation of developing new relationships relevant to your job search that will also lead to additional information, advice, and referrals. These letters will help you build an important contact list from which you should receive additional advice and referrals. In many cases you should be able to turn these letters into telephone and face-to-face interviews – the prerequisites for getting the critical job interview. We include several examples of these networking or approach letters for your reference. In many respects these are the most important types of job search letters you will write. They can be amazingly powerful letters that generate quality job leads that in turn lead to job interviews and offers.

> *An effective job search letter is one that gets read and responded to in positive ways.*

- **Express your thoughtfulness and gratitude for receiving assistance from others.** When was the last time you received a thank you letter? How did it make you feel? Chances are you receive few thank you letters, and those you do receive make you feel good. Furthermore, you remember in a positive way those who write a thoughtful thank you letter; these are nice people. In the case of a job search, you must do more than just communicate your qualifications and potential performance to employers. Your values and personal qualities are also important to others who evaluate individuals according to personal criteria. That's what makes you likable. Most people prefer associating with individuals they like, who demonstrate gratitude for assistance received, and who acknowledge them as a contributor to their success. You express such values when you write thank you letters in which you express your sincere appreciation for others' assistance as well as acknowledge them as a contributor to your present and future success. Sending a well-crafted thank you letter may become the most powerful action you take in your job search.

- **Get invited to job interviews and receive job offers.** Letters oriented toward persuading others to take action on your behalf are usually follow-up or follow-through letters. You send these letters after you have either submitted a resume and/or application or completed a job interview. These letters are expected by the recipient because you mentioned you would follow up. For example, you should include in the cover letter accompanying your resume this type of action statement:

> *I'll call Thursday afternoon, October 20, to see if our schedules would permit a convenient time for us to meet to discuss our mutual interests and my qualifications.*

If you call and are unable to reach this individual, you should send another letter in which you mention your continuing interest in the position and request an interview. This letter also should include another time you will call. You should follow the same procedure in the case of the job interview. As you close, request permission to follow up the interview with a telephone call:

> *If I don't hear from you by next Thursday, would it be okay for me to call your office to check on when you plan to make your final decision?*

This request almost always receives an affirmative response. If you call and learn the decision has not been made, send a follow-up letter mentioning you called and reiterate your interest in the job. Also, state that you will call again to inquire about the hiring decision.

Using Faxes and E-mail

Faxes and e-mail have increasingly supplanted mailed letters as major mediums for distributing communications. They have two major advantages over regular mail – they are cheap and efficient. These are the quickest ways to send messages, and they often result in immediate responses from interested recipients. But they also have one major disadvantage – they may project a poor image of your communication skills. E-mail looks the worst, since you have little control over the format, type style, and overall message presentation. Indeed, you may not know how your message will appear on the recipient's computer.

Unless someone requests that you fax or e-mail them, we still prefer mailing a well-crafted paper letter that observes the rules of good presentation. If you must fax someone, be sure your message is presented in letter form and followed with a mailed copy of the original letter, which better ensures its receipt. If you e-mail a job search letter, make certain you have written a coherent and professional letter, double-checked your spelling and grammar, and included complete contact information: name, address, phone and/or fax number, and e-mail address. E-mail users are notorious for sloppy and unprofessional communication – complete with many spelling and grammatical errors and short, incomplete, and often incoherent sentences. As a result, their e-mail messages tend to be ineffective because they communicate incompetence. Therefore, be very careful in using e-mail in your job search. Do so only if requested, if you know the recipient prefers receiving e-mail, or if the time element is critical.

While many people love e-mail, others are overwhelmed with the many messages they receive daily; they only open and respond to a small percentage of such messages. In fact, many e-mail recipients are increasingly efficient at deleting unwanted or unrecognized messages within a matter of seconds. They seldom open messages from strangers, regardless of the enticing attention lines. When conducting a job search, do not assume faxes and e-mail are more effective than mailed letters. Assume you are a stranger intruding on someone's valuable time. Your message may or may not be read, depending on the situation and recipient. Slow and effective communication is always preferable to fast and ineffective communication.

Letters That Represent the "Unique You"

Whatever you do, make sure you write your own job search letters rather than copy or creatively plagiarize examples of others. The following pages provide examples of outstanding job search letters designed to communicate information and grab the attention of recipients at various stages in any job search. As such, these examples (1) illustrate key writing principles, (2) reveal important strategies, and (3) demonstrate different types of letters that should be written for a variety of occasions.

Make sure your letters represent the "unique you" to others. They should express your style and special qualities. Above all, they should clearly communicate your personality and professionalism. They should indicate that you are an enthusiastic, likable, thoughtful, honest, and competent individual – qualities that are difficult to express in a resume. To do otherwise is to engage in deceptive, unethical, or dishonest job search practices. How you write a letter may indicate to employers how well you will perform on the job – an indicator of your future behavior. In the eyes of employers, your letters are partial predictors of your future performance. If you copy others' examples, chances are you'll find shortcuts to performing your work – behavior employers definitely want to avoid!

> *How you write a letter may indicate to employers how well you will perform on the job – an indicator of future behavior.*

Choose the Right Resources

Each year millions of job hunters turn to career planning books for assistance. Many begin with a general book and next turn to resume and interview books. Others begin with a resume book and later seek other types of job resources, including letter writing books. Some go directly to computer software programs or visit various Internet sites for producing resumes and preparing for job interviews.

If this book represents your first career planning book, you may want to supplement it with a few other key books. Many of these books are available in your local library and bookstore, or they can be ordered directly from Impact Publications (pages 270-271). Most of these resources, along with hundreds of others, are available through Impact's online bookstore and career advice website:

www.impactpublications.com
www.winningthejob.com

These sites also include new titles, specials, downloadable catalogs and flyers, articles, and job search tips for keeping you in touch with the latest in career information and resources. You also can request a free copy of their latest career flyer by sending a self-addressed stamped envelope (#10 business size) to have it mailed to you. Send your request to:

IMPACT PUBLICATIONS
Free Career Flyer
9104 Manassas Drive, Suite N
Manassas Park, VA 20111-5211

Put Dynamite Into Your Communications

The following pages are designed to help you create your own powerful job search letters for all types of job search occasions. They are based on the 52 principles outlined in the next chapter as well as those found in our companion volumes, *High Impact Resumes and Letters*, *Military Resumes and Letters*, and *Dynamite Cover Letters* (Impact Publications).

If you follow our letter writing principles and develop letters similar to ones outlined in this book, you should be able to create powerful job search letters that command the attention and action of key people involved in your job search – from friends to employers. You will be remembered not only for your qualifications but also for being a thoughtful and likable individual who should be hired. In the end, employers hire people they like and want to be associated with. If written and distributed properly, your letters will help communicate this important principle of **likability**. Make sure you incorporate these principles as you create your own set of dynamite job search letters!

> *In the end, employers hire people they like and want to be associated with.*

2

Avoid Mistakes, Follow Key Principles for Success

F EW PEOPLE ARE BORN WRITERS. For many job seekers, writing letters is a laborious task they would rather avoid. Many of them don't know how to get started, what to say, or how to best end their letters. What they need to start, or perhaps jump-start, their job search are some basic writing tips as well as examples of effective letters for different job search situations and occasions.

Writing job search letters follows a well defined process that incorporates key principles of effective writing. Before you begin creating your own letters, let's make sure you have a clear understanding of some major mistakes letter writers make, as well as the letter writing process and associated principles for effective job search letters. This understanding will help you write your own dynamite job search letters that lead to job interviews and offers.

23 Awful Letter Mistakes Job Seekers Make

Job seekers make many mistakes when writing and distributing job search letters. These mistakes can quickly kill what is otherwise an effective job search. They communicate incompetence and signal there may be something wrong with you. The most common mistakes include the following:

1. Fails to communicate a clear purpose. In other words, why should the letter recipient read the job seeker's letter?

10

2. Neglects to link the needs of the recipient with the goals of the writer.

3. Includes boring contents, reflecting similar approaches used in so many other equally boring letters.

4. Looks unprofessional in form, structure, and design.

5. Includes spelling, grammatical, and punctuation errors.

6. Uses awkward language and the passive voice.

7. Overly aggressive, assertive, boastful, hyped, and obnoxious in tone.

8. Appears self-centered rather than job- or employer-centered.

9. Poorly organized, difficult to follow, or wanders aimlessly.

10. Says little about the writer's interests, skills, accomplishments, or what they expect to achieve in the future.

11. Fails to include adequate contact information.

12. Addressed to the wrong person or sent to the wrong place.

13. Dull, boring, and uninspired.

14. Too long.

15. Poorly typed or printed.

16. Produced on cheap and unattractive paper.

17. Writes only cover letters rather than a variety of other equally important job search letters, such as approach and thank you letters, as part of their job search campaign.

18. Uses an inappropriate distribution approach, such as broadcasting a form letter to hundreds of employers, or faxing or e-mailing letters, when posting a personalized letter would be more effective.

19. Closes the letter with the traditional *"I look forward to hearing from you"* rather than specify a follow-up action on the part of the letter writer.

20. Fails to follow up letters within one week with a telephone call.

21. Handwrites letters rather than type them using a letter quality printer.

22. Uses inappropriate stationery and the wrong sized envelope.

23. Does not know how to relate job search letters to other equally important job search activities.

Job search letters that avoid these mistakes may be on the right road to job search success. They at least avoid the trash bin where so many other ineffective job search letters find their final resting place.

The Process

Effective job search letters follow certain principles of effective letter writing, production, distribution, and follow-up. Take special note that we include the elements of **production**, **distribution**, and **follow-up** along with **writing**. For to write a letter without relating it to the next three steps in the letter writing process may effectively kill what was otherwise a perfectly good letter.

While the job search should be viewed as a **process** involving specific steps that lead to job interviews and offers, letter writing also should be treated as a process. This process involves four distinct steps:

1. Writing

The focus here is only on the rules of letter structure, content, and style – good organization, grammar, spelling, punctuation, and tone. These are key writing elements you learned in English classes as a student – how to develop a perfect writing piece. When transferred into the letter medium, the rules of good letter writing also include the use of proper form (full-blocked, square-blocked, modified-blocked, semi-blocked) and structure (heading, date line, inside address, salutation, body, continuation pages, closing, signature line, enclosures, copy reference, postscripts). Given the specific purpose of job search letters – get interviews and job offers – the style and tone of these letters should be closely associated with the style and tone of good advertising copy. Such letters should incorporate these principles of good advertising:

- Catch the reader's attention.
- Persuade the reader about you, the product.
- Convince the reader with more evidence.
- Move the reader to take action (acquire the product).

2. Production

These principles focus on how you will produce your letters. What type of medium will you use? Will you handwrite, type, computer-generate, fax, or e-mail your letters? How neat does the final copy look? What type style will you use? Will you produce the final copy with a letter quality or laser printer? If mailing your letter, what type of paper will use you use? What about the color, weight, size, or cotton content of your paper? Will you use personalized stationery or just a plain piece of paper? If you are e-mailing, how will you address your letter and what type of contact information will you include in it? You need to answer these questions and make corresponding decisions **before** you begin sending your letters to specific persons.

3. Distribution

Distribution is a much neglected principle of letter writing. Most letter writers think all they need to do is to properly fold the letter and drop it in the mailbox. Others prefer faxing or e-mailing their letters. However, you should first address some key distribution questions before ending your letter in this manner. For example, if you are mailing your letters, what size envelope will you use? How will you label the envelope – handwrite or type the address? Are you planning to use any special delivery services, such as overnight or second-day UPS, Federal Express, or Express Mail services? What type of postage will you use – stamps or machine-affixed postage? How do you plan to distribute cover letters? Broadcast them to hundreds of employers or target them on only a few select employers? What about faxing and e-mailing your letters? Are these distribution mediums more effective than the traditional mailed letter?

4. Follow-Up

Follow-up is the key to getting letter recipients to take action. Without follow-up, your letters are likely to result in little or no positive action. You should specify what follow-up actions you will take within a few days after sending your letter. In most cases, follow-up should take the form of a telephone call. It also includes certain types of follow-up letters.

Each of these steps incorporates specific principles that contribute to the job search writing success.

52 Principles for Effectiveness

Several principles make the job search letter process work well for mailed letters. Each of the following 52 principles relates to particular steps in the job search process as outlined on page 4. Treat these principles as a comprehensive checklist for evaluating the effectiveness of your job search letters:

Audience

1. Responds to the needs of my audience as indicated from my research on both the organization and the employer.

2. Presents a unique style in both form and content that will be remembered by the letter recipient.

3. Expresses a **benefit** for the reader that will motivate him to become interested in me and take appropriate action.

Form, Structure, and Design

4. Makes an immediate good impression on the reader and is inviting to read.

5. Properly incorporates the first seven structural elements of an effective letter – heading, date line, inside address, salutation, body, closing, and signature line.

6. Body of letter is subdivided into two to four paragraphs – but no more.

7. Most paragraphs run no more than five lines.

8. Includes complete name and address of letter recipient.

9. Name is signed firmly and confidently using a blue pen.

10. Uses a standard typing style.

11. Has a clean, crisp, uncluttered, and professional look.

12. Uses a 1¼ x 1½ inch margin around the top, bottom, and sides.

Organization and Content

13. Immediately grabs the reader's attention.

14. Presents most important ideas first.

15. Expresses ideas concisely.

16. Relates to the reader's interests and needs.

17. Persuades the reader to take action.

18. Free of spelling, grammatical, and punctuation errors.

19. Incorporates the active voice.

20. Avoids negative words and tone; uses positive language throughout the letter.

21. Expresses the "unique you" rather than merely approximate the language and content of model letters.

22. Employer-centered rather than self-centered.

23. Stresses benefits the reader is likely to receive from you.

24. Demonstrates a clear purpose.

25. Sentences and paragraphs flow logically and with proper transitions.

26. Includes complete contact information (avoid Post Office box numbers in lieu of a street address).

27. Expresses enthusiasm, energy, and fire.

28. Follows the ABC's of good writing – <u>A</u>lways <u>B</u>e <u>C</u>lear, correct, complete, concise, courteous, considerate, creative, cheerful, careful.

Production

29. Has an overall strong professional appearance sufficient to make an immediate favorable impression.

30. If typed, uses a new or nearly new ribbon (if cloth) with clean keys or printer head. If word-processed, use a letter quality printer (no dot matrix). If e-mailed, follows key letter composition principles.

31. Copy setting adjusted properly so the final copy is not printed too dark or too light.

32. Printed with a standard type style and size.

33. Produced on a letter quality machine.

34. Proofread and ran "spell check" (if using a word processing program) and proofread again for possible spelling/typing errors. Read and reread for errors if composing an e-mail message.

35. Used a good quality paper that looks and feels professional.

36. Selected a paper color appropriate for audience.

37. Compared to most business letters received over the past year, this is one of the best in appearance.

Distribution

38. Addressed to a specific name and complete address.

39. Inserted into a No. 10 business or a 9 x 12 inch envelope.

40. Checked to make sure all enclosures were indeed enclosed.

41. Matched the envelope paper stock and color to the stationery if mailed in a No. 10 business envelope.

42. Typed address and return address.

43. Affixed a commemorative stamp.

44. Used a special delivery service for overnight delivery in cases where this attention-getting action seemed appropriate.

45. Affixed a U.S. Postal "Priority Mail" sticker on the envelope if mailed in an envelope larger than a No. 10 business envelope.

46. Faxed letter only if requested to do so; mailed a hard copy labeled "Faxed" along with date and time of transmission.

47. E-mailed letters and messages if appropriate for the situation.

Follow-Up

48. Ended letter with an "action statement" indicating you would contact the individual by phone within the next week.

49. Made the first follow-up call at the time and date indicated in your letter. If using e-mail, follow up all unanswered e-mail messages within 48 hours with another e-mail message attached to the same message asking if the recipient received the first transmission.

50. Followed up with additional phone calls until you were able to speak directly with the person or received the requested information.

51. Maintained a positive and professional attitude during each follow-up activity even after repeated phone calls failed to get through to the letter recipient. You were pleasantly persistent and tactful during all follow-up calls. Never indicated you were irritated, insulted, or disappointed in not having your phone calls returned.

52. Followed up the follow-up by sending a thank you letter genuinely expressing your appreciation for the person's time and information.

All of these principles are elaborated on, including specific examples complete with internal and external evaluation forms, in our other letter writing book, **Dynamite Cover Letters** (Impact Publications).

Whatever you do, make sure your letters have the power to persuade others to take action to your benefit. You can do this if you go beyond the writing stage and incorporate the principles of production, distribution, and follow-up in your job search letters.

Letters for All Job Search Occasions

The 201 job search letters appearing in the following pages are designed for all types of job search occasions and situations, from initiating job research to following up with thank you letters. Regardless of your writing and distribution mediums (mail, fax, e-mail), you can and should write many of these letters at various stages in your job search.

We urge you to examine these letters for ideas on how you can develop the **form and content** of your own job search letters that best represent the "unique you." In each example we've attempted to adhere to our principles of effective letter writing. Please keep in mind there is nothing magical about these examples. They only stress the first stage of letter effectiveness – writing for good form and content. Our examples emphasize how and what to say to individuals in your job search network rather than how, when, where, and with what consequences you will deliver your messages to others. The other stages of letter effectiveness – production, distribution, and follow-up – are the keys to moving your letters into the hands of the right people who will take action that leads to job interviews and offers. It's these other stages that constitute the additional steps you will need to take as you breathe new life into your job search through the letter writing process.

You will encounter many individuals and occasions for writing a variety of job search letters. The nine most common occasions include:

1. Letters to start your job search.

These letters effectively kick off your job search into fruitful directions. Your goal at this initial stage should be to gather useful information for developing an effective job search. At this stage you need to contact a variety of groups and individuals: organizations as sources of information on potential employers; organizations as potential employers; publications with job listings; employment services; groups having information on relocation; and organizations with job search resources. These letters may request annual reports, subscription services, contractual services, relocation information, and books. Responses to these letters should help create a solid database for launching an effective job search.

2. Letters that help lay the ground work for future job search success.

You also need to write several letters for developing important relationships that will hopefully promote your job search. These letters inform others of your job search intentions and activities. They let others know you are in the process of looking for a job, that you welcome advice and referrals, and that you would appreciate that some of your contacts serve as personal and professional references. You address these letters to friends, relatives, acquaintances, professional colleagues, former employers, professors, teachers, ministers, and others who might be willing to serve as a reference or who can provide you with information, advice, or referrals for building your job search network. Many of these letters result in making direct contact with potential employers.

3. Letters for developing contacts, uncovering job leads, and acquiring useful information and advice.

The purpose of these letters is to make direct contact with employers for information, advice, referrals, and job interviews. These are the most important "networking" letters you will write. You write many of these letters based on referrals from other individuals. You should also write "cold turkey" letters – those written directly to employers without the benefit of referrals. Taken together, these letters become the most powerful job search letters you can write for getting a job interview and offer.

4. Letters that respond to classified ads and job vacancy announcements.

These letters address the specific job qualifications and requirements outlined in employers' vacancy announcements. They may or may not accompany a resume. Most of these letters are classic cover letters – they provide "cover" for a resume. While these are the most frequently written job search letters, they also are some of the most ineffective letters. The most effective such letters, especially "T" letters, directly respond to position requirements as well as include follow-up actions.

5. Cover letters.

These letters always accompany resumes. They respond to employers' hiring needs as well as clearly highlight the interests and qualifications of the candidate. In essence, these letters provide "cover" for resumes.

6. Resume letters.

These letters are written in lieu of sending a traditional resume and cover letter. They combine the best elements of both a resume and cover letter in a single letter format.

7. Follow-up letters.

In many respects these may be the most effective job search letters you will ever write during your job search. They are designed to get employers to take action in reference to your job search activities.

8. Thank you letters.

These, too, are some of the most effective job search letters you will ever write. They communicate an important quality employers seek – thoughtfulness. As a result, they set you apart from other job seekers who fail to write such letters. Thank you letters should always be sent to individuals who have provided assistance, be it in the form of information, advice, referrals, or an actual job interview.

9. Special and unusual letters.

A variety of other letters may also be sent during different stages of your job search. Many of these are written for special occasions – offering a solution to an employer's problem, for example. Many are unusual letters that are aimed at getting the attention and action of potential employers. They are unusual for both their medium and message. For example, some of these letters may arrive in the form of a telegram, a formal invitation, a photo-card, an accompanying video, or a card attached to a bouquet of flowers, poster, or a shoe box. But be aware that these are risky letters – they may kill your chances of getting an interview!

Put Sizzle In Your Letters

The following chapters are organized according to these various types of job search situations and letters. The examples are based upon the principles outlined earlier in this chapter. We urge you to examine each of these examples in terms of their communication principles and content. When it comes time to write job search letters, make sure your letters reflect the "unique you" – your personality, professionalism, and enthusiasm. Whatever you do, avoid creating "canned" letters that were merely edited, or "creatively plagiarized," from such examples. Be sure to demonstrate that your skills and accomplishments fit the employer's needs. Letters that emphasize what you, the job candidate, can do for the employer create the type of sizzle that moves employers to take positive action.

3

Key Letters for Starting Your Job Search Right

GETTING STARTED ON YOUR job search can be a difficult task. Where do you start? What should you do? Whom should you contact? These questions can easily be answered by thinking about what needs to be done **first** in order to launch a successful job search. By doing first things first, you will put in motion a proper sequence of activities that will enhance your job search success.

Gather Useful Information

While some job seekers think they first need a resume or job interview, what they really need is good **information** about the job market, employers, organizations, jobs, job searches, relocation considerations, and resources for managing their job search. While much of this information can be accessed by telephone, well crafted letters will go a long way in launching a successful job search at this initial stage.

Information-gathering letters should be short and to the point. You need not dwell at length about your goals and qualifications. After all, you are seeking information – not a job – at this stage. If you use the Internet, you'll want to search several websites for job-related information. Most employers, for example, have their own websites, which often reveal important information on their operations and personnel. The more information you can gather on the Internet, the better. At this stage of the job search we prefer sending e-mail whenever possible, because it is fast and has a much higher probability of being

22

responded to than traditional mailed letters. If you are not familiar with e-mail and job-related Internet sites, we highly recommend the following books which will quickly put you in contact with many useful sites for job information, networking contacts, and job listings:

**100 Top Internet Job Sites**, Kristina M. Ackley (Impact Publications)

**America's Top Internet Job Sites: The Click and Easy™ Guide to Finding a Job Online**, 2nd Edition, Ron and Caryl Krannich (Impact Publications)

**Adams Internet Job Search Almanac** (Adams Media)

**Cyberspace Job Search Kit**, Fred E. Jandt and Mary B. Nemnich (JIST Publishing)

**Career Exploration on the Internet** (Ferguson Publishing)

**Guide to Internet Job Searching**, Margaret Riley Dikel and Frances Roehm (McGraw-Hill)

**Haldane's Best Employment Websites for Professionals**, Bernard Haldane Associates (Impact Publications)

**Job Searching Online for Dummies, With CD-ROM, 2nd Edition**, Pam Dixon (Wiley & Sons/IDG)

Many of these resources are available in bookstores and libraries or can be ordered directly from Impact Publications (see order form at the end of this book or visit their online bookstore: www.impactpublications.com).

An Effective E-mail Approach

When using e-mail, pay particular attention to what you put in the subject line to get the attention of the recipient. The word "QUERY" in caps is often a good choice for requesting information or action. For example, you might include this subject line when asking for information about an association's membership directory, a subject that appears in our first letter example on page 26:

Subject: QUERY – membership directory information

The word "QUERY" indicates that you are primarily seeking information rather than trying to sell something, a frequent subject of spam and other unsolicited e-mails to companies, organizations, or individuals. You'll also be able to quickly identify responses to such e-mails when the recipient replies to your "QUERY" message using the same subject line.

Keep It Short and to the Point

Most of these letters can be completed in a few sentences and paragraphs. Keep in mind that your reader is probably a busy person who readily has the information you need. Make his or her job easy by making your request simple and to the point. In some cases you may want to telephone for the information rather than write a letter. Whatever your medium of choice, you still need to gather important job search information **before** sending cover letters and resumes to potential employers.

Letters to start your job search may be aimed at six different information sources. These include letters addressed to:

- Organizations as sources of information on potential employers.

- Organizations as potential employers.

- Publications with job listings and other job information.

- Job search, employment, and career assessment services.

- Groups offering relocation information and services.

- Organizations with job search resources.

Taken together, these "starter" letters identify numerous groups you should consider contacting at the very beginning of your job search. Most will help give direction to your job search. Others emphasize the importance of using group resources in developing an effective job search. And others potentially put you in contact with employers. If you examine the contents of these letters, you should get several useful ideas on how to best organize your job search.

A good way to get your job search launched is to write 25 or more of these letters. The writing exercise itself will help you focus your job search on initial information needs and direct it into fruitful channels. For example, where do you want to live and work during the next five years? If you are considering a move from Boston to Seattle, you need to gather information on your targeted community. What's the job outlook like in Seattle? We know it's good right now. Who are the major employers in Seattle? What's it like living and working there? Will you have problems finding housing? What's the cost of living in Seattle? What are the long-term economic forecasts for this community?

If you are staying close to home, you still need to gather information on potential employers. If you are unfamiliar with a business or an organization, write for a copy of their annual report or for other literature on the organization. Contact local employment services to find out what type of services they offer and at what cost and with what performance guarantees. If you need assistance with your job search – from acquiring books to being given a battery of assessment tests – write letters to get this type of information.

The letters presented in this chapter are designed for these six types of initial job search situations. The contents of each outline particular job search needs.

Requesting Information
(membership listings)

124 Linden Place
Chicago, IL 60002

October 2, 20____

Mindi Mason, Director
ENVIRONMENTAL RESEARCH CENTER
147 Gilbert Avenue
San Francisco, CA 91441

Dear Ms. Mason:

I'm in the process of researching various organizations involved in conducting environmental research on tropical rainforests. Specifically, I'm trying to identify the types of research being conducted as well as the size and location of the various research organizations.

As the national association of environmental research firms, would you have such information available in the form of a membership directory or report?

I would appreciate any assistance you might be able to provide on this subject. Please let me know if there is any charge for this service. Should you wish to contact me by telephone, my number is 312/371-6651.

Sincerely,

Steven Wallace

Steven Wallace
wallaces@mylink.com

Requesting Information
(placement services)

853 West Norton Road
Boise, ID 88344

July 8, 20_____

Director
Information Services
ASSOCIATION OF
    AMERICAN ACCOUNTANTS
5391 Tyler Road
Washington, DC 20543

Dear Director:

Does your association provide information on job vacancies with member organizations? As a recent graduate in accounting, I'm interested in contacting firms which are members of your association for employment information.

If you do offer placement services, or publish a newsletter that includes vacancy information, I would appreciate hearing from you. Please send me the necessary information for using your services.

Thank you for your assistance.

Sincerely,

George Miles

George Miles
milesg@mylink.com

Requesting Information
(alumni network)

973 West End
New York, NY 10001
February 13, 20____

Wanda Evans, Director
Alumni Services
UNIVERSITY OF
       SOUTHERN CALIFORNIA
1933 Jasper Street
Los Angeles, CA 90312

Dear Ms. Evans:

I've been working in New York City with an investment banking firm
since graduating from USC in 1992. I'm now in the process of
conducting a job search in the Houston area.

I would like to make more contacts with individuals working in and
around Houston. Is there a USC alumni group in Houston or does
your office have a listing of USC alumni currently residing there?

I would appreciate any assistance you could give me in making contact
with fellow alumni. I'm especially interested in acquiring information
on job opportunities in the international investment banking field.

Many thanks for your assistance. I look forward to hearing from you.

Sincerely,

Brenda Carpenter

Brenda Carpenter
carpenterb@mylink.com

Requesting Information
(placement services)

325 Davidson Drive
Baltimore, MD 23153
February 4, 20____

Editor
ASSOCIATION TRENDS
18 St. Elmo Drive
Bethesda, MD 22332

Dear Editor:

I understand you provide a placement and referral service for your subscribers and readers. In reviewing previous editions of your publication, I learned this included an "Availability Announcement" section along with a resume referral service.

If you still provide this service, I would appreciate information on procedures and costs for being included in the service. Please send me the information as soon as possible since I want to be included in the next issue.

Thank you for your assistance.

Sincerely,

Janice Forbes

Janice Forbes
forbesj@mylink.com

Requesting Information
(placement services)

246 Cathedral Drive
Salt Lake City, UT 86732

June 3, 20____

James Martin
Association Referral Service
U.S. CHAMBER OF COMMERCE
1615 H Street, NW
Washington, DC 20062

Dear Mr. Martin:

I recently learned your office provides placement information and services for your member organizations. I'm especially interested in employment opportunities in Western Europe.

Could you please send me information on your placement services, including any forms I would need to complete and applicable fees?

I appreciate your assistance.

Appreciatively,

Sandra Vertimosa

Sandra Vertimosa
vertimosas@mylink.com

Requesting Publications/Data
(targeting job search)

1134 Jackson Place
Sacramento, CA 95243

November 15, 20____

Wilson James, Director
Office of Procurement
Procurement Support Division
AGENCY FOR INTERNATIONAL
    DEVELOPMENT
1100 Wilson Blvd., 14th Floor
Rosslyn, VA 20523

Dear Mr. James:

I understand you now have available the latest editions of the <u>Current Technical Service Contracts and Grants</u> and <u>AID-Financed University Contracts and Grants</u> directories which list all contracts and grants awarded to contractors, nonprofit organizations, and educational institutions by AID during the past three years. I also understand you produce the quarterly <u>Functional Report: Current Indefinite Quantity Contracts</u> report.

I would appreciate it if you could send me the latest editions of these three publications. I know these were previously available at no charge. Should there be a charge, please let me know as soon as possible since it is urgent that I receive them.

Thank you for your kind assistance.

Sincerely,

Martin Grant

Martin Grant
<u>grantm@mylink.com</u>

Requesting Company's Annual Report
(via one's stockbroker)

831 Old Town Blvd.
St. Louis, MO 64210

April 7, 20_____

John Wilson
SMITH, GRAY, AND WILSON
714 Jefferson Ave., Suite 120
St. Louis, MO 64313

Dear John,

I'm in the process of making a job change and thought you might be able to assist me in gathering information on a firm I'm interested in pursuing – J.C. Williams Company. I know they are listed on the American Stock Exchange.

I would like to know something about the financial outlook of this company. Would it be possible to get me a copy of their annual report as well as any other information on this organization? Who knows, we might decide to buy some stock in the company!

Many thanks for your assistance.

Sincerely,

Mary Stafford

Mary Stafford
staffordm@mylink.com

Requesting Information on Company
(direct contact)

4439 Center Street
Portland, OR 98211
January 30, 20____

Melanie Roberts, Director
Public Relations Office
TRC PHARMACEUTICAL COMPANY
1000 West Knight Street
Terre Haute, IN 48732

Dear Ms. Roberts:

I'm in the process of conducting research on various pharmaceutical companies as part of a career development project. Your company was highly recommended as one of the leaders in the field.

Could you please send me information on your company, including an annual report as well as any other information that would help me better understand the future direction of your company? I'm especially interested in learning about your operations in Columbia, Missouri. I enclose a mailing label for your convenience.

Thank you for your assistance.

Sincerely,

Jeffrey Williams

Jeffrey Williams
williamsj@mylink.com

Requesting Vacancy Announcement
(government agency)

1156 P Street, NW
Washington, DC 20037

December 20, 20_____

Fred Teposo
Bureau of Indian Affairs/MS-331 SIB
Branch of Personnel Services/Code 675
1951 Constitution Avenue, NW
Washington, DC 20245

Dear Mr. Teposo:

In reviewing this week's issue of the <u>Federal Job Opportunities Listing</u>, I learned you had a vacancy for a Highway Engineer, GS-810-11/12.

Could you please send me a copy of the vacancy announcement (#EAO-90-19) for this position as well as any other information that outlines application procedures? I enclose a mailing label for your convenience.

Thank you for your assistance.

Sincerely,

John Alabroso

John Alabroso
alabrosoj@mylink.com

Requesting Information
(subscription)

325 Park Avenue
Indianapolis, IN 47721

August 23, 20____

Manager
Subscription Department
TOLEDO DAILY NEWS
117 S. 47th Street
Toledo, OH 41153

Dear Manager:

I'm planning to move to the Toledo area within the next six months. In preparation for the move, I would like to subscribe to the Sunday edition of the Toledo Daily News which I believe has the most complete weekly listing of employment and real estate classifieds.

Could you please let me know what the subscription procedure and cost would be to receive the Sunday edition? I would like to begin my subscription immediately.

Thank you for your assistance.

Sincerely,

Elizabeth Martino

Elizabeth Martino
martinoe@mylink.com

Requesting Relocation Information

9341 Capitol Street
Omaha, NE 54371

March 3, 20_____

Director
Relocation Department
CENTURY 21
9431 Sheridan Road
Austin, TX 77211

Dear Director:

I will be relocating to the Austin area within the next eight months. Could you send me information on Austin as well as your relocation services?

I'm especially interested in purchasing a home in the $250,000-300,000 range in an area with excellent public schools. I would appreciate any information you could provide me with on both the housing situation and the Austin community.

Sincerely,

Janice Wilson

Janice Wilson
wilsonj@mylink.com

Requesting Information

(relocation)

882 Timberlake Road
Minneapolis, MN 54371

February 7, 20_____

Janice Watson
FIRST CENTURY REAL ESTATE
792 North Adams St.
Suite 319
Knoxville, TN 38921

Dear Ms. Watson:

We plan to move to the Knoxville area within the next six months. Please send us information on your services as well as sample copies of current listings. We would also appreciate any information on Knoxville that would help us better understand the community, such as a directory of churches, schools, and community activities.

We're especially interested in finding a neighborhood with good schools and recreational facilities. We are prepared to look in the price range of $225,000 to $275,000. While we prefer buying, we also would consider renting with an option to buy.

We look forward to working with you in the coming weeks.

Sincerely,

Steven Pollock

Steven Pollock
pollocks@mylink.com

Requesting Relocation Information
(international)

7741 Cedar Lane
Bethesda, MD 20931

May 11, 20____

Janice Lawrence, President
INTERNATIONAL EXPATRIATES
781 Washington Blvd.
Boston, MA 02112

Dear Ms. Lawrence:

I will be moving to Italy within the next six months. In visiting a friend recently, I learned about your wonderful publication – <u>The International Expatriate</u> – for expatriates residing in Europe.

Could you please send me order information on this and any other publications you may have for assisting me with our relocation? We're especially interested in learning more about the schools and employment opportunities in and around Milan.

I appreciate your assistance and look forward to hearing from you.

Sincerely,

Marsha Ventura

Marsha Ventura
<u>venturam@mylink.com</u>

Entering Subscription
(community jobs newspaper)

382 Vancouver Blvd.
Seattle, WA 99311

April 21, 20____

Subscription Manager
THE EMPLOYMENT PAPER
329 2nd Avenue West
Seattle, WA 98119

Dear Subscription Manager:

Could you please enter my subscription for six biweekly issues of
The Employment Paper? I enclose a check for $30 to cover the
cost of the subscription.

I look forward to receiving my first issue.

Sincerely,

Martin Yost

Martin Yost
yostm@mylink.com

Entering Subscription
(federal jobs listing service)

2201 State Street
Albuquerque, NM 83210

August 22, 20____

Circulation Manager
FEDERAL RESEARCH SERVICE
P.O. Box 1059
Vienna, VA 22180

Dear Circulation Manager:

I'm in the process of conducting a job search with the federal government. I understand you publish a biweekly listing of federal job vacancies, offer computer software for completing the OF-612, and conduct job search seminars.

Please send me information on how I can subscribe to Federal Career Opportunities. I'm interested in the six-week subscription. I would also appreciate information on any of your other products and services.

Thank you for your assistance.

Sincerely,

Steven Willow

Steven Willow
willows@mylink.com

Requesting Subscription
(international jobs newspaper)

930 West 21st Street
Albany, NY 19999

April 23, 20____

Subscription Manager
INTERNATIONAL
      EMPLOYMENT GAZETTE
1525 Wade Hampton Blvd.
Greenville, SC 29609

Dear Subscription Manager:

Your publication was highly recommended in the new edition of <u>The Complete Guide to International Jobs and Careers</u>. I'm enclosing a check for $35 to cover the cost of a six-issue subscription. I would appreciate it if you could send me my first issue as soon as possible.

I also understand you operate an international resume writing and referral service. Could you please send me information on this service? I'm particularly interested in finding employment with an accounting firm operating in Europe or the Middle East.

Thank you for your assistance.

Sincerely,

Eileen Young

Eileen Young
<u>younge@mylink.com</u>

Requesting Subscription
(international education/job listings)

9124 Harrison Blvd.
Providence, RI 02412

August 7, 20____

Subscription Manager
THE INTERNATIONAL EDUCATOR
P.O. Box 103
West Bridgewater, MA 02379

Dear Subscription Manager:

Please enter my one-year subscription to <u>The International Educator</u>. I enclose a check for $30 to cover the cost of the four-issue subscription.

Also, please send me the free 16-page booklet – "TIE'S Complete Guide to Finding a Job in an International School" – which comes with my subscription. I'm anxious to get my international job search underway as soon as possible.

Thank you for your assistance.

Sincerely,

Mary Davis

Mary Davis
<u>davism@mylink.com</u>

Developing Connections
(long-distance employers)

771 West Nelson St.
Denver, CO 80121

May 14, 20____

President
CHAMBER OF COMMERCE
444 State Avenue
Phoenix, AZ 89921

Dear President:

I will be moving to the Phoenix area soon. I would appreciate it if you could send me a directory of your members. I'm especially interested in making contact with retailers who are the major employers in your community.

Thank you for your assistance.

Sincerely,

Stephanie Adams

Stephanie Adams
adamss@mylink.com

Requesting Resources
(job search directory/catalog)

5187 Terrace Blvd.
Dayton, OH 43281

December 17, 20_____

Publisher
IMPACT PUBLICATIONS
9104 Manassas Drive, Suite N
Manassas Park, VA 20111-5211

Dear Publisher:

I recently learned about your resource guide, "Job, Career, and Hiring/Retention SuperSource," which includes more than 1,300 career resources. I understand this publication is available free of charge.

Could you please send me a copy as soon as possible? I also would like order information on your book, High Impact Resumes and Letters. If you accept credit card orders, please include your fax number so I can place my order by fax.

Sincerely,

Stanley Johnson

Stanley Johnson
johnsons@mylink.com

Requesting Order Information
(job search book)

6613 Stevens Point
Detroit, MI 46821
June 1, 20____

Publisher
IMPACT PUBLICATIONS
9104 Manassas Drive, Suite N
Manassas Park, VA 20111-5211

Dear Publisher:

I've been trying to locate a copy of <u>High Impact Resumes and Letters</u> in my local bookstore but with no success. Could you please send me this book as soon as possible since I'm in immediate need of this book for developing my job search?

I enclose a check for $24.95 ($19.95 plus $5.00 shipping) to cover the cost of this book. Please let me know if this is the correct current price. I've been using the older 1990 edition which I found in our local library.

Sincerely,

Alice Bolton

Alice Bolton
<u>baltona@mylink.com</u>

Requesting Services
(resume production)

8004 Teasley Court
New Haven, CT 03982

November 21, 20____

Marilyn Jones
FAST RESUMES
421 New York Avenue
New Haven, CT 03980

Dear Ms. Jones:

I understand your company offers resume writing and production services. Could you please send me information on your services so I will have a better idea of how I could best use them?

Since I'm in the process of revising my resume, I would like to know if your company would be able to further strengthen my resume. I enclose a sample copy for your reference.

I specifically need to know the cost for your services and how long it would take before I would have camera-ready copy. Also, do you produce the final copy with matching stationery for cover letters?

I look forward to hearing from you. My phone number is 203-771-8920. You also can contact me by e-mail: henryg@mylink.com.

Sincerely,

Henry Greystone

Henry Greystone
henryg@mylink.com

Request for Subscription/Referral Services

113 Bellflower Ct.
Orono, ME 08013

August 9, 20_____

Subscription Manager
ACCESS: Networking in the
    Public Interest
50 Beacon Street
Boston, MA 02108

Dear Subscription Manager:

I understand you publish a biweekly listing of vacancies with nonprofit organizations as well as offer related job search services to individuals interested in jobs with nonprofit organizations.

I'm interested in reviewing your current vacancy announcements, but I'm not sure where I can gain access to your database. Which libraries or nonprofit organizations in the Orono, Maine area subscribe to your service? I would appreciate it if you could send me information on these organizations. I would also appreciate information on your job matching services, which I understand is available on a fee basis to individuals.

Thank you for your assistance.

Sincerely,

Stacy Chino

Stacy Chino
chinos@mylink.com

Requesting Information/Registering
(temporary employment services)

1134 Stanford Lane
Orlando, FL 31339
July 11, 20_____

Janice Eaton
HIGH TEMPS
73 Weston Road
Suite 913
Orlando, FL 31341

Dear Ms. Eaton:

I am interested in a temporary position in word processing. As my enclosed resume indicates, I have over seven years of progressively responsible experience working with a variety of software programs. During the past three years I have extensively used the newest versions of Word.

Could you please send me information on how I might work with your organization? I assume you have signed contracts with those who register with your firm. Please send me information about your organization as well as the necessary forms for registration.

I would appreciate it if you could keep my resume on file for future reference. Should a position become available for someone with my experience, I would like to hear from you.

I will give you a call next week to answer any questions you might have concerning my interests and background.

Sincerely,

Martin Davis

Martin Davis
davism@mylink.com

Requesting Job Search Services

5431 Atlanta Blvd.
Atlanta, GA 33479
May 9, 20____

Thomas Allen
CAREER BEST ASSOCIATES
848 Peachtree Plaza
Atlanta, GA 33481

Dear Mr. Allen:

I am in the process of making a career change. During the past seven years I have worked in the field of education as a Speech Therapist. I'm interested in leaving education to pursue a career in the private sector.

A friend recommended that I contact you concerning your career transition services. She mentioned you were one of the leading firms providing such career assistance.

I would appreciate it if you would provide me with information on your services. I especially need to know how you operate with clients, including career counseling, testing, and placement services. I would like to know what types of contractual arrangements I would be entering for what period of time, the costs of your services, and how many job interviews and offers I might expect during the contract period.

I would also appreciate it if you could provide me with the names and telephone numbers of three former clients who have successfully used your services.

I enclose a copy of my resume for your reference. I have a strong teaching and research background which I need to relate to jobs and careers outside education. Please let me know if the services of your company would be appropriate for someone with my background.

Sincerely,

Paul Martinez

Paul Martinez
martinezp@mylink.com

Contacting Executive Search Firm

1367 River Run Dr.
Burke, VA 23222

September 17, 20_____

Maryann Philips
EXECUTIVE SEARCH UNLIMITED
821 Shore Drive
Suite 913
Miami, FL 32193

Dear Ms. Philips:

I understand you specialize in recruiting chemical engineers in the international environmental field. During the past five years I have worked with the Environmental Protection Agency as a policy analyst in its Office of International Affairs. I've had a unique opportunity to apply chemical engineering skills to important international policy issues.

I plan to leave government for the private sector within the next 18 months. I'm interested in the possibility of working with an international contracting and consulting firm in the environmental field. Since this is an area in which you recruit, I would appreciate it if you could keep my resume on file for future reference.

Please let me know if you need any additional information on my background and availability.

Sincerely,

Debra Follett

Debra Follett
follettd@mylink.com

Contacting Resume Database Service

752 Thompson Court
Albany, NY 14321

March 23, 20____

James Reston
HEALTH SYSTEMS RECRUITERS
918 Monroe Street
Chicago, IL 60021

Dear Mr. Reston:

Mary Allen suggested that I send you a copy of my resume. She said you specialized in recruiting health care administrators for HMOs.

I have nine years of progressive experience in administering two medium-sized health care facilities in upper New York State. Within the next two years I hope to relocate to the Southwest, preferably a major metropolitan area in Arizona or Southern California.

I enclose a copy of my resume for your reference. Mary Allen also mentioned you maintain a resume bank of potential candidates for your clients. I would appreciate it if you could keep me on file for future reference.

Please let me know if you need any additional information.

Sincerely,

Doris Luffert

Doris Luffert
luffertd@mylink.com

Screening Employment Services

8801 West End St.
Cleveland, OH 45313

December 29, 20____

President
JOBS ABROAD
203 Ocean Blvd.
Ft. Lauderdale, FL 31111

Dear President:

I noticed your ad in the <u>Cleveland Plain Dealer</u> for information on job opportunities in Australia. I'm curious as to what you have to offer, since I understand the current unemployment rate in Australia is nearly 15 percent.

I would appreciate it if you could send me information on your product or service. If you are one of the firms selling a video accompanied by a listing of Australian employers, or if you require up-front fees for promised job placements, please do not reply to this letter. I'm only interested in contacting a bona fide firm that is retained by employers.

Sincerely,

Daryl Peterson

Daryl Peterson
petersond@mylink.com

Contacting Potential Employer
(resume bank)

452 North Belmont
Franklin, KY 42012
October 23, 20____

Gerald Davidson
Agricultural Education Services
2314 23rd Street, NW
Washington, DC 20123

Dear Mr. Davidson:

I'll complete my Ph.D. in agricultural economics from the University of Kentucky within the next six months. While conducting my dissertation research in the Philippines last year, I met two of your staff members who were working from your Davao City regional office – Steven Chambers and Allan Able. They suggested I send you a copy of my resume for your reference.

I understand you maintain a resume bank you refer to for candidates to staff upcoming projects. I would like to be included in it as well as considered for future projects relating to the Philippines or other countries in which you work.

I'm especially interested in developing marketing systems relating to irrigation cooperatives. My dissertation research has focused on the role of revolving funds in irrigation cooperatives as they relate to developing new agricultural marketing mechanisms for developing countries. This is an area the World Bank and the Agency For International Development have indicated a strong interest in developing pilot projects in fifteen countries during the next five years.

I would appreciate an opportunity to discuss with you and your staff how my work might be developed into new project proposals for these organizations. I'll call your office next Thursday to see if you have any questions concerning my background and interests.

Sincerely,

Sandra Alliston

Sandra Alliston
allistons@mylink.com

Requesting Information
(testing and assessment services)

891 Davis Blvd.
Austin, TX 71311

September 4, 20____

Janet Evans, President
CAREER TESTING SERVICES, INC.
234 Warner Drive
Austin, TX 71312

Dear Ms. Evans:

I'm in the process of re-entering the job market after ten years as a homemaker. When I attended high school nearly 20 years ago, I took a battery of tests to determine my occupational interests, skills, and abilities. I'm sure my interests, skills, and abilities have changed considerably since that time.

I understand you administer similar tests that are more current and perhaps more useful for today's job market. Could you send me information on what types of testing services you offer, including your fee schedule?

Thank you for your assistance.

Sincerely,

Martha Vestal

Martha Vestal
vestalm@mylink.com

Requesting Information
(job search services)

8901 Taylor Road
Birmingham, AL 32112

April 2, 20_____

Alice Steves, Director
THE WOMEN'S CENTER
7742 Federal Avenue
Birmingham, AL 32114

Dear Ms. Steves:

I learned from a recent article in the <u>Daily News</u> that you offer job and career assistance. Since I've been out of the job market for several years, I'm really interested in learning about job alternatives for someone with my background. I also need to get a better idea of what I'm best qualified to do as well as how to write a resume.

Could you please send me information on the services available through your center? For example, do you offer individualized testing and assessment services and courses on how to write resumes and interview for jobs? I would be interested in knowing how I can best use the Women's Center for conducting a job search.

I appreciate your assistance and look forward to working with you and your staff.

Sincerely,

Janice Furniss

Janice Furniss
furnissj@mylink.com

Requesting Information

(job search assistance)

882 West 23rd Street
Kansas City, MO 64444

May 11, 20____

Jill Mason, Director
40-PLUS OF KANSAS CITY
1133 Truman Blvd.
Kansas City, MO 64444

Dear Ms. Mason:

I will shortly become unemployed because my company, where I've worked for nearly 20 years, decided to relocate to Florida. I'm now in the process of looking for an executive level position with a company in the Kansas City area.

One of my close friends highly recommended that I contact you. She found her current job while participating in your group several years ago.

I understand you provide a variety of job search services for individuals in my situation. Could you please send me information on your organization and how I might participate? Since my last day of work will be next Friday, I'm prepared to conduct a job search on a full-time basis. Any assistance 40-Plus of Kansas City could give me would be greatly appreciated.

Sincerely,

David Fortina

David Fortina
fortinad@mylink.com

Requesting Job Search Assistance

1134 West Ford Ave.
Dallas, TX 73112

August 14, 20____

Dr. Delores Clements
DALLAS COMMUNITY COLLEGE
Career Counseling Center
241 Lone Star Blvd.
Dallas, TX 73110

Dear Dr. Clements:

A friend informed me that your Center offers a variety of job search courses and services that are open to the general public.

I've been unemployed during the past three months. So far my efforts at landing a job have not been successful. At this point I think I need some professional guidance to help get my job search on track.

Could you send me information on what types of courses and services you offer? I probably need some testing and assessment work. And I know I could use some assistance on improving my resume.

Sincerely,

Martin Morrison

Martin Morrison
morrisonm@mylink.com

Requesting Information
(career training and placement services)

722 Georgetown Road
Washington, DC 20134

February 18, 20_____

Director
SATO TRAVEL ACADEMY
1005 N. Glebe Road
First Floor
Arlington, VA 22201

Dear Director:

I saw your ad in yesterday's edition of <u>The Washington Post</u>. I'm interested in pursuing a career in the travel industry, preferably with one of the major airlines.

Could you please send me information on your training programs? I'm especially interested in learning more about the duration and costs of training as well as your placement services.

I look forward to receiving information on your programs.

Sincerely,

Nina Barton

Nina Barton
<u>bartonn@mylink.com</u>

4

Laying Essential Ground Work for Future Success

WHILE THE LETTERS IN Chapter 3 were primarily designed to gather information for directing your job search into fruitful channels, the examples in this chapter help develop important relationships for conducting an effective job search. Most of these letters are addressed to people you know but who may not be aware you are in the process of looking for a job. These letters represent important job search activities you should engage in at the very beginning of your job search. They are an important set of networking letters that should help generate useful information, advice, and referrals for directing your job search.

Contact Helpful People

One of your first job search activities should be to contact individuals who may be helpful to you in looking for employment. These individuals may include friends, relatives, acquaintances, professional colleagues, former employers, professors, teachers, ministers, or other people who might serve as either a professional or personal reference or who may be able to provide you with information, advice, or referrals relevant to your job search. These also include your college placement office. You want to let these people know you are in the process of looking for a job. You just never know what might come of these letters. Some of these contacts might refer you to an employer who is seeking someone with your experience and qualifications.

Gather References

At the very start of your job search you need to begin thinking about persons you want to ask to serve as your references. After all, some time during your job search, usually during the job interview, you will be asked for references. While many employers never check these references, others will. Make sure the individuals you designate as your references know about your job search. They should be informed that you are looking for a job as well as the type of job and employer you are seeking. They should have a copy of your resume on file along with a letter that outlines your plans and asks permission to use them as a reference. You should also keep them informed of your job search progress. If you know you are likely to be interviewed for a job, let them know about the specific job so they have some idea of the type of position you will be seeking. The more information you can provide them on your goals and the specific position, the better prepared they should be to give you a strong recommendation, if the prospective employer calls them.

Announcing Your Intentions

The process of developing contacts and job leads or networking involves contacting numerous people. One of the most important groups for developing your networks consists of individuals you already know. These may include the following people:

- Friends (take a look at your Christmas card list)

- Neighbors (current and past)

- Social acquaintances: social club members, tennis, golf, swim, PTA members

- Classmates – from any level of school

- College alumni (get a list of those living near you)

- Teachers – your college professors, your children's teachers

- Relatives – include distant relatives who may not be on your Christmas card list

- Anybody you wrote a check to in the past year:

  - tradespeople, drugstore owner
  - doctor, dentist, optician
  - lawyer, accountant, real estate agent
  - insurance agent, stockbroker, travel agent

- Manager of local branch of your bank

- Present and former co-workers

- Politicians (local leaders often are businessmen/women or professionals in town who seem to know everybody)

- Chamber of Commerce executives in town

- Your pastor, minister, rabbi, or other clergy (excellent resource)

- Members of your church

- People you meet at conventions

- Speakers at meetings you've attended

- Business club executives and members (Rotary, Kiwanis, Jaycees)

- Representatives of direct-sales business (real estate, insurance, Amway, Shaklee, Avon)

- Delivery people (UPS, FedEx, Postal Service)

After developing your comprehensive list of contacts, classify the names into different categories of individuals. Remember, each individual has his or her own network of contacts that may be helpful in developing your job search campaign. These include:

- Those in influential positions or who have hiring authority.

- Those with job leads.

- Those most likely to refer you to others.

- Those with long-distance contacts.

Select at least 25 names from your list for initiating your first round of contacts. In your letters to these individuals, inform them of your job search intentions and request assistance in the form of advice and referrals. In so doing, you will initiate your prospecting and networking campaign, which hopefully leads to several informational interviews, formal job interviews, and job offers. These letters may well become your most important job search letters. They give direction to the core dynamics for finding jobs on the hidden job market – prospecting and networking.

While some of these letters will be accompanied by a resume – primarily for the recipient's reference – many networking letters should not include a resume. To do so would be to violate a key principle of networking – asking for a job rather than requesting information, advice, and referrals. You usually present your resume at the very **end** of a face-to-face informational interview. Your letter should be the primary vehicle for opening doors in your networking campaign. We'll examine several networking letters, commonly referred to as "approach letters," in Chapter 5.

Express Your Sincere Gratitude

Be sure to write thank you letters any time someone assists you with your job search. These letters should be routinely sent when someone gives you advice or referrals or indicates their willingness to serve as a professional or personal reference. These letters communicate your **thoughtfulness** to others – one of the most important qualities you should continuously express throughout your job search. Thank you letters can make the difference between receiving active advice and referrals or getting only perfunctory "best wishes with your job search" responses. Indeed, many job seekers and employers report thank you letters to be more important to getting a job than other types of job search letters.

Requesting Information
(organizing placement files)

248 Buchanan St., Apt. 201
Flint, MI 48321
September 21, 20____

Susan Strousburg, Director
Career Planning and Placement
UNIVERSITY OF DETROIT
Detroit, MI 47315

Dear Ms. Strousburg:

I'm a 1999 graduate of the University of Detroit with a B.S. in biology. During the past two years I've worked in several part-time positions. I'm now in the possess of seeking a full-time position, preferably with the pharmaceutical industry.

I anticipate contacting numerous employers and interviewing for several positions during the next three months. However, I believe I need to update my placement file since several changes have taken place during the past three years.

Could you send me the necessary forms for updating my file? I probably need to include new references. Also, does your office provide job search assistance for alumni? If so, what type of assistance might I receive? I'll call your office next week to check on my file and these questions.

I appreciate your assistance.

Sincerely,

Jeffrey Taylor

Jeffrey Taylor
taylorj@aol.com

Requesting Reference
(former teacher)

9113 Stanford Road
Milton, PA 18722
January 4, 20____

Professor Martin Stone
Department of English
UNIVERSITY OF PITTSBURGH
Pittsburgh, PA 17231

Dear Professor Stone:

It has been nearly three years since we last discussed the role of creative writing in business communication. I remember so well your advice on developing other-directed goals in all forms of communication. It has helped me on numerous occasions to better organize thoughts and messages in my daily work – even though I've spoken more Spanish than English during the past two years!

Since completing my BA three years ago, I joined the Peace Corps and served as a Volunteer in Guatemala. I taught English as a foreign language in a small high school near Guatemala City and even helped develop an English club which became popular in our community. Three of my students did so well that they are now foreign exchange students in the States.

While I very much enjoyed my Volunteer experience, I must now turn my attention to more long-term career concerns. As you can see from my enclosed resume, I'm hoping to find a high school English teaching position – preferably in the Philadelphia area.

I would appreciate it if you could serve as one of my references. I enclose a reference form requested from the university placement office. Could you please complete this form and return it to the placement office as soon as possible? I enclose a self-addressed stamped envelope for your convenience.

I really appreciate your assistance with this matter. I'm hoping to have my placement file complete within the next two weeks and shortly thereafter begin interviewing for positions. Should you hear of any vacancies for someone with my qualifications, please feel free to pass my name and resume on to interested parties.

I hope to be in the Pittsburgh area sometime next month. Perhaps we could get together briefly over a cup of coffee. I'm anxious to learn what's been happening in the department during the past three years.

Sincerely,

Janet Stillman

Janet Stillman
stillmanj@erols.com

Requesting Reference/Contact
(former employer)

643 Nellum Street
Knoxville, TN 34822
April 9, 20____

Susan Jacobson, President
JACOBSON AND TYLER ADVERTISING
239 Wabash Street
Chicago, IL 60003

Dear Susan,

Since leaving Chicago three years ago, I've been working for a small advertising company here in Knoxville – J. C. Thompson. I've very much enjoyed the work. Indeed, I've done some of my most creative work during these past 18 months.

I will be re-entering the job market within the next six months. My present employers have decided to retire after nearly 30 years of business. Since the local economy has negatively impacted advertising, it does not appear the firm will be sold to an outside investor. Consequently, we are all preparing to say "Goodbye." At the same time, I've decided to move to Seattle to be closer to my parents who are now in their mid-80s. I'll be seeking a position in advertising in the Seattle Metro area.

I immediately thought of you as I began planning for this move. I remember how helpful you were in connecting me with my current position, for which I am very grateful. Could I again call on you for advice and assistance?

- Do you know anyone in the Seattle-Vancouver area who might be interested in my background?

- Could I use your name as a reference?

I enclose a copy of my resume for your information. Please feel free to pass it on to anyone who might be interested in my qualifications.

Will you be attending the National Conference on Media Advertising in San Francisco next month? Marilyn and I will be there for four days, (May 15-18). We'll be staying at the Omni International. It would be great to see you again and perhaps get together for lunch or dinner. Marilyn says she knows some wonderful seafood restaurants you'll just love!

Sincerely,

Bill McDonald

Bill McDonald
mcdonaldb@ace.com

Requesting Reference
(minister)

7231 Delaware Street
Winston-Salem, NC 39482
March 19, 20____

Rev. George C. Allen
CHURCH OF CHRIST
984 Angelical Avenue
Winston-Salem, NC 39482

Dear Rev. Allen:

As you may know, I will be graduating from Central High School in
June. In September I will attend the University of North Carolina in
Chapel Hill where I plan to major in dental hygiene. Between June and
September I'm hoping to land a summer job that will enable me to save
money for next year's college expenses.

Would you be so kind as to serve as a personal reference? Since I have
very little work experience, potential employers will probably want to
know something about my personal character. I thought of you as a
reference because I've been very active in our church youth group. I
believe you more than anyone else have had a chance to observe me
working with others.

I appreciate your assistance. Should an employer ask for a reference, I
will give them your name and telephone number.

Sincerely,

Margaret Davis

Margaret Davis
margaretdavis@earthone.net

Informing About Job Search/
Requesting Advice and Referrals

711 W. End Street
New York, NY 10023
January 4, 20____

Darlene Mason
213 Camelback Road
Phoenix, AZ 89241

Dear Darlene,

I just received our alumni bulletin and noticed you now live in Phoenix. What a coincidence. My husband John and I will be moving to Phoenix in April. His company, Sontana Electronics, transferred him to their Phoenix research center.

It will be good to see you again and catch up on the last ten years of our lives. I always remember our late night dorm sessions when be talked at length about what we were going to do when we graduated. Now we should have some really good stories!

I'm sure you could give us some great "Phoenix" tips. One of my major concerns will be looking for a job. During the past five years I have been working part-time as a management trainer. Now that our children are in school, I plan to look for a full-time training position. Should you know of firms that hire for such positions, I would appreciate learning about them. I'm trying to make as many contacts as possible with potential employers before we make the move in April.

We're really looking forward to our move to Phoenix – and seeing you again.

Sincerely,

Margaret Benton

Margaret Benton
bentonm@aol.com

Informing About Job Search/ Requesting Advice and Referrals

203 Jason Drive
Columbia, MO 67332
July 2, 20____

Janice Peterson
Guidance Department
JEFFERSON COUNTY HIGH SCHOOL
492 West County Road
Columbia, MO 68221

Dear Ms. Peterson:

Nearly four years have passed since I last saw you. I remember how helpful you were when I was trying to decide on my career direction.

As you know, I joined the U.S. Navy immediately after graduation. I've had a chance to learn a great deal during this time, from becoming a communications specialist to having a chance to travel to many parts of Europe and the Middle East. It's been a very interesting and rewarding four years.

I'll be leaving the Navy in another six months. My plans are to return to Columbia and get a job. I'm also hoping to attend junior college on a part-time basis. I eventually want to get my degree in computer science.

I'm really not sure where to start my job search in Columbia. Do you have any suggestions? I enclose a draft of my resume for your reference. Perhaps you know some employers who might be interested in my qualifications. I would appreciate any leads you are able to share with me.

I look forward to seeing you again when I return to Columbia.

Sincerely,

Margaret Snyder

Margaret Snyder
snyderm@erols.com

Informing About Job Search/ Requesting Advice and Referrals

GERALD S. SNYDER   Email: snyderg@earthweb.net
782 South Street ■ Seattle, WA 98322 ■ 802-/731-9228

August 3, 20____

John Turner
STATE FARM INSURANCE
993 Colony Terrace
Seattle, WA 98321

Dear John,

I wanted to let you know that I'm in the process of changing jobs. I'm leaving R.J. Systems after four years of increasingly responsible sales and marketing experience. Jane and I plan to remain in Seattle.

Do you know of any employers in the Seattle area that would be interested in my sales and marketing background? Perhaps you might have some suggestions as to whom I might contact. I enclose a copy of my resume for your reference.

I'll give you a call next week.

Sincerely,

Gerald Snyder

Gerald Snyder
geralds@planet2.com

Expressing Gratitude for Reference

481 Alliance Street
Milford, MA 02189

February 21, 20____

Professor Stanley Friar
Department of Engineering
UNIVERSITY OF MASSACHUSETTS
Amherst, MA 03192

Dear Professor Friar:

Thank you so much for helping me complete my placement file. The placement center informed me that my file is now complete. I know you are very busy, and completing recommendation forms is quite time consuming.

I'm sure your recommendation will assist me greatly with my job search. In fact, my first job interview is scheduled for next week. I'll be interviewing for an entry-level position with R.C. Jameson, Inc., a Boston-based engineering firm specializing in urban mass transit design. They are doing the type of work I'm most interested in pursuing at this initial stage of my career.

I'll keep you informed on my progress.

Sincerely,

April Carter

April Carter
cartera@aol.com

Expressing Gratitude for Job Search Advice

9912 Cortney Place
Bethesda, MD 20999
March 2, 20____

Sarah Allison
839 P Street, NW
Washington, DC 20032

Dear Sarah,

Thanks so much for your advice on contacting professional associations
for editing opportunities in the publishing industry. Concentrating
primarily on local newspapers and magazines, I hadn't thought of these
groups as "publishers."

What a pleasant surprise it was to discover that several associations
headquartered in Alexandria, Virginia, operate huge publishing programs. They produce monthly newsletters and magazines with circula-
tions in excess of 500,000 as well as operate large book publishing
divisions. Best of all, many are regularly seeking editing talent.

I've contacted several associations in the Washington, DC area during
the past few days. The ones that most interest me are doing exciting
work in the health care and environmental areas. I'm developing some
good contacts with these organizations that I hope will turn into job
interviews.

Without your advice I would have overlooked what appear to be some
of country's major publishers. Thanks for helping me re-direct my job
search focus. I'll keep you posted as to where all this leads.

Sincerely,

James Patterson

James Patterson
pattersonj@ace.com

Expressing Gratitude for Job Referral

8123 Park Avenue
Albuquerque, NM 84913

May 17, 20____

Vivien Parker
452 Albert Street
Albuquerque, NM 84909

Dear Vivien,

You were right! Margaret Easton knows her stuff. What a wonderful person to meet and learn from.

She was really helpful in giving me advice on whom to contact for possible job openings in the paralegal field. She also shared some of her "inside" observations on which firms I should avoid. I did not know, for example, that several major law firms are currently reducing their staffs.

She suggested that I focus my job search on a few small law firms specializing in environmental law. It's a growing legal area I'm very interested in. She made some good suggestions on how I could best strengthen my resume for such firms. She also referred me to three firms which I've contacted; two will interview me next week.

I enclose a copy of my revised resume for your reference. I think it better represents my goals than the one I gave you a few weeks ago.

Thanks again for recommending that I contact Ms. Easton for information and advice. She may be responsible for my landing my next job!

Sincerely,

Janice Davidson

Janice Davidson
jdavidson@hotmail.com

5

Developing Contacts and Job Leads

HOW DO YOU PLAN TO approach employers? What strategies and techniques will you use to communicate your qualifications to them? Will you primarily respond to want ads and vacancy announcements with cover letters, resumes, and "T" letters, or will you make cold telephone calls or directly contact employers with unsolicited resumes and letters?

In this chapter we examine several letters used for approaching employers. Whereas application and cover letters primarily respond to want ads or vacancy announcements, approach letters are usually not written with a particular job vacancy in mind. Their purpose is to **develop contacts** which may or may not lead to useful information, advice, and referrals. Eventually many of these letters pay off by making contacts with employers who have jobs appropriate for your interests, skills, and abilities.

Powerful Approach Letters

Approach letters are some of the most powerful job search letters you will ever write. While most job seekers are preoccupied with writing cover letters to accompany resumes, few job seekers ever write approach letters. These letters are so important that we recommend you spend at least 35 percent of your writing time producing approach letters. They become your calling card for opening the doors to potential employers.

Networking Nuts and Bolts

Approach letters build and extend job search networks; networks are the key to uncovering jobs that best fit your interests, skills, and motivations. They are the job search equivalent to the prospecting and networking activities engaged in by salespeople to expand and build their client base. You will expand and build your networks by writing and following up the many approach letters you should write throughout your job search.

Approach letters communicate your interests, skills, abilities, and motivations to others – who may or may not be potential employers – in a low-keyed manner. In contrast to cover letters and resumes that basically ask for a job, approach letters primarily seek information, advice, and referrals. These are non-threatening letters since they do not put individuals on the spot by asking them for a job.

> *Approach letters primarily seek information, advice, and referrals.*

Two Basic Forms

Approach letters come in two basic forms – cold turkey and referral. **Cold turkey approach letters** are the written equivalent to a cold telephone call. These letters are written to individuals without the benefit of a prior contact. The best such letters attempt to find some common ground from which to link the writer's interests and goals to those of the letter recipient.

Referral approach letters are written with the benefit of a contact person. You link yourself to the letter recipient by way of someone he or she knows and hopefully respects. Depending on the quality of the referral, this contact person may result in instant access to the letter recipient, who feels obligated to grant you an informational interview or at least give you information, advice, and referrals over the telephone. In other cases the referral is for the purpose of identifying a possible job opening.

The major purpose of both types of approach letters is the same – get information, advice, and referrals from the letter recipient. Information, advice, and referrals are the key elements for building job search networks that lead to employers who have the type of job you are looking for. If you fail to write these letters, you will neglect one of the most fruitful avenues for uncovering job leads and landing the right job for you.

We also include examples of approach letters that are aimed at possible job openings. Written as either cold turkey or referral approach letters, these letters go beyond the less subtle information and advice gathering letters. They frankly ask the letter recipient if he or she has or knows of a job opening for someone with your interests, skills, and experience. The cold turkey version of these types of approach letters is similar to cold telephone calls used by salespeople engaged in prospecting for new clients.

Role of Resumes

Examine the following letters carefully. Keep in mind the clear purpose of each letter – acquire useful information, advice, and referrals rather than arrange a job interview or ask for a job. Unfortunately, many writers of approach letters get confused about their purpose and thus make the mistake of putting the letter recipient on the spot by asking for a job. Furthermore, many writers enclose their resume with these letters – a clear sign they are confused about what they are doing. Regardless of what you

> *A resume should never accompany an approach letter.*

say in your letter, an enclosed resume indicates you are looking for a job. The resume, in effect, turns the approach letter into a cover letter. It weakens the impact of the approach letter and thus effectively kills it as a networking device.

A resume should never accompany an approach letter. In this situation the resume is best shared with the letter recipient at the end of a face-to-face informational interview. This interview should be the ultimate goal of your approach letter – schedule a meeting wherein you interview the individual to gain information, advice, and referrals. It is only at the very end of this interview that you should share your resume with the individual and ask him or her to critique it. In addition to gaining important information, advice, and job lead referrals, your approach letters should eventually result in an improved resume. It will reflect the thoughtful advice received from those who granted you an informational interview.

For more information on the role of letters and resumes in networking activities as well as the informational interview, see two of our other career books – *The Savvy Networker* and *Interview for Success*.

Taking Action

Similar to other job search letters, approach letters require you to take initiative in contacting the letter recipient for a meeting. Make sure you end your letter with a statement concerning what **action** you will take next and when the person can expect to hear from you. In most cases referral approach letters will result in scheduling a face-to-face meeting. Expect nearly 50 percent of cold turkey approach letters to result in either a face-to-face meeting or a telephone conversation with the letter recipient. If you mistakenly enclose your resume with an approach letter, expect your response rate to decline dramatically. Despite what you say in your letter about only seeking information and advice, a resume accompanying an approach letter says *"I'm looking for a job – do you have one?"* Few people are interested in spending valuable time talking to applicants who ostensibly approach them for information and advice but who apparently only want to "use" them for getting a job.

Referral
(information and advice)

1099 Seventh Avenue
Akron, OH 44522
December 10, 20____

Janet L. Cooper, Director
Architectural Design Office
RT ENGINEERING ASSOCIATES
621 West Grand Avenue
Akron, OH 44520

Dear Ms. Cooper:

John Sayres suggested that I write to you regarding my interest in architectural drafting. He thought you would be a good person to give me some career advice.

I am interested in an architectural drafting position with a firm specializing in commercial construction. As a trained draftsman, I have six years of progressive experience in all facets of construction, from pouring concrete to developing plans for $14 million in commercial and residential construction. I am particularly interested in improving construction design and building operations of shopping complexes.

Mr. Sayres mentioned you as one of the leading experts in this growing field. Would it be possible for us to meet briefly? Over the next few months I will be conducting a job search. I am certain your counsel would assist me as I begin looking for new opportunities.

I will call your office next week to see if your schedule permits such a meeting.

Sincerely,

John Albert

John Albert
jalbert@hotmail.com

Cold Turkey
(information and advice)

2189 West Church Street
New York, NY 10011

May 3, 20___

Patricia Dotson, Director
NORTHEAST ASSOCIATION
    FOR THE ELDERLY
9930 Jefferson Street
New York, NY 10013

Dear Ms. Dotson:

I have been impressed with your work with the elderly. Your organization takes a community perspective in trying to integrate the concerns of the elderly with those of other community groups. Perhaps other organizations will soon follow your lead.

I am anxious to meet you and learn more about your work. My background with the city Volunteer Services Program involved frequent contact with elderly volunteers. From this experience I decided I preferred working primarily with the elderly.

However, before I pursue my interest further, I need to talk to people with experience in gerontology. In particular, I would like to know more about careers with the elderly as well as how my background might best be used in the field of gerontology.

I am hoping you can assist me in this matter. I would like to meet with you briefly to discuss several of my concerns. I will call next week to see if your schedule permits such a meeting.

I look forward to meeting you.

Sincerely,

Carol Timms

Carol Timms
ctimms@yahoo.com

Referral

(information and advice)

235 W. Charles Street
Baltimore, MD 21200
July 26, 20___

Craig Allen
T. ROWE PRICE ASSOCIATES, INC.
100 East Pratt Street
Baltimore, MD 21202

Dear Mr. Allen:

Jerry Weitz recommended that I contact you about my interests in Graphic Design. He spoke highly of you and said you might be able to give me some useful advice on job opportunities for someone with my background and interests.

Two years ago I completed my bachelor's degree in Graphic Design. Since then I've been working as a graphic designer at L.C. Printing Company where I've acquired invaluable experience in all phases of graphic design and production. I have a working knowledge of offset printing and have worked extensively with the Word, PageMaker, and QuarkXPress software.

Mr. Weitz said you have been working with one of the country's leading investment firms during the past seven years as a publications oriented graphic designer. I'm interested in learning more about career opportunities with corporations seeking to develop in-house graphic design capabilities. Would it be possible to meet briefly to discuss my career interests? Since my experience has been limited to the printing industry, I'm sure I could learn a great deal from you.

I'll call you on Wednesday afternoon to see if your schedule would permit such a meeting. I really appreciate whatever information and advice you could give me.

Sincerely,

Laura Baker

Laura Baker
laurabaker@ivillage.com

Cold Turkey
(information and advice)

136 West Davis Street
Washington, DC 20030
October 2, 20___

Sharon T. Avery
Vice President for Sales
BENTLEY ENTERPRISES
529 W. Sheridan Road
Washington, DC 20011

Dear Ms. Avery:

I am writing to you because you know the importance of having a knowledge-able, highly motivated, and enthusiastic sales force market your fine information processing equipment. I know because I have been impressed with your sales representatives.

I am seeking your advice on how I might prepare for a career in your field. I have a sales and secretarial background – experience acquired while earning my way through college.

Within the coming months I hope to begin a new career. My familiarity with word processing equipment, my sales experience, and my bachelor's degree in communication have prepared me for the information processing field. I want to begin in sales and eventually move into a management level position.

As I begin my job search, I am trying to gather as much information and advice as possible before applying for positions. Could I take a few minutes of your time next week to discuss my career plans? Perhaps you could suggest how I can improve my resume – which I am now drafting – and who might be interested in my qualifications. I will call you on Monday to see if such a meeting can be arranged.

I appreciate your consideration and look forward to meeting you.

Sincerely,

Gail S. Topper

Gail S. Topper
topperg@aol.com

Referral
(information and advice)

SAMUEL ROLLINS
rollinss@planetnow.net

---

782 N. Davis   Raleigh, NC 27832   831-782-4813

June 28, 20____

Janet O'Brien
JAMES, ALLEN, AND O'BRIEN
8132 Broadway
Washington, DC 20031

Dear Ms. O'Brien:

Mary Varner recommended that I contact you concerning my plans to relocate to the Washington, DC area. She said you would be a good person to talk with concerning my interests in contacting firms specializing in environmental law.

While completing my law degree at Emory University, I became very interested in environmental law. Many of the cases I reviewed involved law firms, lobbyists, nonprofit environmental groups, and federal agencies located in Washington, DC. Not surprisingly, I concluded the nation's capital is obviously the center for anyone interested in pursuing a career in environmental law.

I'll be visiting Washington the week of July 23. Would it be possible to get together briefly to discuss my career interests. I know I could learn a great deal from your experience and would appreciate any information, advice, and referrals you might give me on opportunities in environmental law. I'll call you next Thursday to see if your schedule would permit such a meeting.

I look forward to meeting you.

Sincerely,

Samuel Rollins

Samuel Rollins

Cold Turkey
(information and advice)

MARTIN L. POTTER   E-mail: *mlpotter@hotmail.com*

632 Old Gates Road   Landover, MD 23219   410-392-9231

March 17, 20___

Thomas Nelson
ACT TRAINING SYSTEMS
719 Wilson Blvd.
Arlington, VA 21313

Dear Mr. Nelson:

As a fellow member of the American Society for Training and Development, I've admired your work in expanding the involvement of technical trainers in our local ASTD chapter. Indeed, our April symposium on "Developing Needs Assessment in Technical Training" was one of the most useful meetings I've ever attended. It gave me several new ideas I've been able to incorporate in my own professional development.

During the past five years I've been working as a technical trainer with the Department of the Navy. I specialize in computer programming of communication systems. While I've very much enjoyed my work with the Navy, it's now time I begin looking at career options in the private sector. I'm especially interested in working with a small consulting firm – preferably one doing contract work with the government – specializing in technical training.

Would your schedule during the next few weeks permit a few minutes to meet with me to discuss my career interests? Having been out of the job market for several years, I would value your advice on how I might best approach the private sector with my technical training interests and skills.

I'll call your office on Thursday afternoon to see if such a meeting would be possible.

Sincerely,

Martin L. Potter

Martin L. Potter

Cold Turkey
(information and advice)

9231 Taylor Avenue
Cincinnati, OH 43821
February 3, 20___

Marsha Sullivan, Director
COMMUNITY ACTION FOR SENIORS
812 Fairview Blvd., Suite 201
Cincinnati, OH 43820

Dear Ms. Sullivan:

Congratulations on receiving the annual Jaycees' Community Service Award for your work in developing recreational facilities for the elderly. I've been especially impressed with the new recreational center you helped develop at Siedler Park. It's been a wonderful success, one which many other communities should look to for new ideas.

I'm writing to you because you are experienced in working with the elderly on recreational issues. During the past three years I've been completing my master's degree in social work while teaching full-time at Wallace High School. I'm planning to leave teaching next year to pursue a career with community-based programs for the elderly.

My long-term career interests are in gerontology. While working on my master's thesis – "Recreational Options for the Elderly: A Comparison of Three Innovative Community Programs" – I became very interested in working with local recreation programs. I'm now committed to pursuing a career relating to recreation and the elderly.

I would appreciate an opportunity to speak with you about your work in this field. At this stage I'm trying to learn as much as possible about career opportunities relating to recreation involving the elderly. Perhaps you could advise me on where and how I should best focus my job search during the next year.

I'll call your office next week to see if your schedule would permit a brief meeting to discuss my career interests. I would appreciate any information, advice, or tips you might provide me at this time.

Sincerely,

Margaret Allen

Margaret Allen
allenm@yahoo.com

Cold Turkey
(possible opening)

5680 Citrine Blvd.
Pekin, IL 61559

March 1, 20____

John Dingle
General Manager
PEORIA GAZETTE
13 Walsh Street
Peoria, IL 61564

Dear Mr. Dingle:

I have five years experience as the Personnel Director at the Pekin Times.
I have learned a great deal and contributed much during that time, and
now would like to move to a position with a larger organization. While at
the Times, I have learned specifically about personnel situations that are
unique to the publishing business. It is for that reason that I would like to
move to another news organization even though I realize that my personnel experience could be useful in many other businesses as well.

The Pekin Times has been a leader in personnel innovations, which have
enabled me to put into place new policies that have been credited with
increasing productivity and cutting costs while maintaining customer
satisfaction. Highlights of my accomplishments include:

- Cost savings of 20% in medical premiums by instituting programs to improve employee health.

- Reduction of 18% in employee turnover by more carefully
  screening job applicants and training new employees.

- Reduction of 11% in employee absenteeism through a coordinated effort to respond to employee complaints by both
  Personnel and Department Managers.

I would appreciate the opportunity to talk with you about the directions
in which you are headed at the Peoria Gazette. Whether or not we find
that there might be an opportunity for me to work in your organization in
the future, I think a meeting could be productive for both of us.

I will call you next week to schedule a meeting at your convenience.

Sincerely,

Jack Fielding

Jack Fielding
jackfielding@ace.net

Cold Turkey
(possible opening)

327 Saffron Court
Pensacola, Fl 33218
January 8, 20____

Darlene Textron, Editor
HONOLULU STAR BULLETIN
87 Lafayette Square
Honolulu, HI 96829

Dear Mrs. Textron:

For the past two years I have been a copywriter for the <u>Pensacola News-Journal</u>. I have found my time in this position to be both productive and enjoyable. I love writing for the newspaper!

I will be making a permanent move to Honolulu in early April and hope to continue to work in the news department for a major newspaper. I believe the <u>Honolulu Star Bulletin</u> would be a good fit for my interest and skills. As you can see from the resume I enclose, I was graduated from the University of Missouri with a double major in journalism and communication. The combination of my formal training with the excellent experience I have had at the <u>Pensacola News-Journal</u> has provided me with a solid background to become a contributing member of another news team. I have been fortunate here to have had the opportunity to work with and learn from some of the best news people in Florida. In fact, I was honored to be awarded the certificate of achievement as best copywriter in Northwest Florida at our regional meeting last month.

I will visit Honolulu early next month to make arrangements for housing and also plan to make contacts with various news organizations. I would like very much to talk with you about possible opportunities with the <u>Honolulu Star Bulletin</u>. I realize that you may not have a position open at present, but I believe it could be in the best interests of both of us to explore possible avenues that might be open in the future.

I will call you next week to see whether we might be able to meet briefly while I am in Honolulu. I will truly appreciate any time you could take from your busy schedule to meet with me. I feel sure I would benefit from having the opportunity to talk with you about the newspaper business in Hawaii.

Sincerely,

Phyllis Jourdan

Phyllis Jourdan
<u>pjourdan@planet2.com</u>

Cold Turkey
(information and advice)

4183 Waupelani Drive
State College, PA 16808

October 26, 20____

Dr. Harold Selnik, Chairman
Department of Speech Communication
UNIVERSITY OF PITTSBURGH
Pittsburgh, PA 12511

Dear Dr. Selnik:

I was fortunate to have been in the audience this past May when you gave the keynote speech at the Speech Communication Association Convention. Not only did your talk hold the entire audience spellbound, but I found your analysis of the future direction of our field to be the most insightful I have encountered.

I am completing the requirements for my Ph.D. in Communication at Penn State and will be graduated in May. I have not yet decided whether I would prefer to teach or use my background in Communication in another arena. Having heard you speak, I am certain your insights would be helpful to me as I consider this decision.

I will be in Pittsburgh over the Thanksgiving holiday. I hope that your schedule will permit you to meet briefly with me during that time. In fact, I could arrange my schedule to be in Pittsburgh a day before or after your holiday break at the University of Pittsburgh if that would be more convenient for you.

I will call you next week. I hope we can schedule a meeting at a mutually convenient time. I value your opinions and feel certain that talking with you will enable me to better plan my future in communication.

Sincerely,

Julie McGuire

Julie McGuire
mcguirej@aol.com

Referral

(information and advice)

4563 Southshore Drive
Key Biscayne, FL 33455

April 15, 20___

Marlo Sikes
Public Relations Director
DOLPHIN CRUISE LINE
873 North American Way
Miami, FL 33132

Dear Ms. Sikes:

Mr. Gerald Barnes of the CruiseLine Travel School, where I am a student, suggested I contact you for information regarding careers in the cruise industry. I will be completing my course work here next month and am seeking information about opportunities in the travel industry in general and the cruise lines in particular. Mr. Barnes indicated you are one of the best sources of information as to the directions the cruise business is taking and that your network of persons involved in the business is the best of any around.

I realize your schedule is hectic, but I hope you will be able to help me by taking a half-hour of your time to meet with me to share your valuable information and insights into the cruise business with me.

I will call you next Monday to arrange a meeting at a time convenient for you. I truly will appreciate your assistance at this important juncture in plotting my future career.

Sincerely,

Miriam Jordan

Miriam Jordan
mjordan@hotmail.com

Referral
(possible opening)

9855 Little Glen Court
Dallas, TX 75207

June 23, 20____

Ida Stonewall
PACIFIC DESIGN CENTER
7008 Melrose Avenue
Los Angeles, CA 90069

Dear Ms. Stonewall:

A mutual friend of ours, Tina McGreggor at the Southwest Interior Design Center in Phoenix, suggested I write to you.

I have just completed the requirements for my MBA degree from the University of Texas. As an undergraduate I had the opportunity to work as a co-operative education student in the administrative offices of the Dallas Design Center. I enjoyed my work there and want to explore the possibility of combining my business management training with my interest in design.

I will be returning to my family's home in Santa Monica next month. Tina indicated you would be one of the best people I could talk to regarding the kind of opportunities in the Los Angeles area for someone who was interested in employment in one of the area design centers. She said your overview would help get me pointed in the right direction!

I will call you next week to see whether we could schedule a meeting during the week of July 10th. I would truly appreciate it if you could take time out from your busy schedule to meet with me.

Sincerely,

JoAnne McGrosney

JoAnne McGrosney
mcgrosneyj@erols.com

Referral

(possible opening)

485 High Bluff Road
Santa Fe, NM 89543
October 3, 20____

Rebecca Lyons
WESTERN INDUSTRIES, INC.
98347 W. Main Street
Albuquerque, NM 89977

Dear Mrs. Lyons:

Cynthia Pringle, my current supervisor and one of your acquaintances, suggested I write to you. I will be relocating to Albuquerque within the next six weeks and will be looking for employment as a secretary. Cynthia indicated your firm is frequently in need of dependable and competent people to fill vacancies.

I have worked for Cynthia for the past three years and have consistently received "outstanding" ratings in all areas on my performance evaluations. I get along well with people and look forward to beginning work in a new firm in my new city.

I will be driving into Albuquerque the week of the 15th and hope I might be able to meet with you at that time. Even if you do not have a vacancy or anticipate one at this time, I would appreciate the opportunity to talk with you about other contacts I might make to further my job search in Albuquerque.

I will call you next week and hope we may be able to schedule a meeting. I will appreciate any assistance you may be able to give me and look forward to meeting you. Cynthia speaks so highly of you that I know your assistance would be truly valuable to me.

Sincerely,

Karen Jostney

Karen Jostney
kjostney@yahoo.com

Referral
(possible opening)

650 Candlestick Lane
Orem, UT 80933
February 11, 20___

Jack Daniels
SUCCESS SEMINARS, INC.
19788 Expert Lane
Provo, UT 81566

Dear Mr. Daniels:

Jeff Holser, one of your former instructors, suggested that I contact you. He indicated that since your firm has been experiencing rapid growth, you would be a logical person for me to talk with regarding possible training opportunities with Success Seminars, Inc.

After teaching writing courses at Brigham Young University for eight years, I resigned to conduct training seminars for Write To The Point, Inc. and have been with them for the past three years. I like the travel opportunities involved in conducting training seminars across the country and enjoy working with the adult participants who enroll in their courses.

After twenty-five years offering training seminars, Write To The Point will be closing its doors since its owner is retiring from the business and has chosen to close rather than sell the business. Hence I am looking for opportunities to put my skills to work with another training firm. Jeff has spoken highly of your firm and the outstanding work that you do.

Some of my accomplishments with my present employer include:

- Rated as "outstanding" instructor by 92% of seminar participants.

- Increased sales of audio tapes and books at seminars by over 50%.

- 62% of participants who attend my seminars sign up for another seminar within six months.

I would appreciate the opportunity to talk with you about your organization as well as possible ways we might work together. I will call you next Monday to schedule an appointment at a mutually convenient time. Thank you for your consideration.

Sincerely,

Bruce Italk

Bruce Italk
italkb@earthme.com

6

Responding to Vacancy Announcements

I F YOU ARE LIKE MANY JOB SEEKERS, you will spend much of your job search time responding to classified ads and job vacancy announcements with letters and resumes. While this approach may not be the most effective for finding a job, nonetheless, it is one important strategy that does lead to real jobs. Millions of jobs are announced in newspapers, magazines, and trade journals and posted on numerous bulletin boards and websites each year.

What type of letter will you write? What should it say about you in relation to the job vacancy? Will it represent your best writing effort? These and several other important questions are addressed in the sample letters appearing in this chapter.

Letters Required

Job vacancy announcements come in many forms and include different types of instructions. Some may ask you to apply in person, which means you must complete an employer's application; you also may be interviewed at the same time. Other announcements may ask you to telephone for further information, which means you will experience a telephone screening interview prior to being contacted by an employer for a face-to-face interview. Others may ask you to send a resume and letter or complete an application. And still others may ask you to fax or e-mail your resume. But most vacancy announcements require you to submit a letter and/or a resume.

Most responses to job vacancy announcements should include a letter. If you must submit a resume via the mail or by fax, be sure to include a cover letter. A resume submitted without an accompanying letter is likely to become a weak resume. The letter is analogous to a headline for advertising copy. It should be designed to grab attention and create interest in you and your resume. It enables you to express your personality, enthusiasm, and unique style – important hiring criteria which are difficult to express in a formal resume. It also should include the most important element in your job search at this stage – a follow-up statement specifying what action you will take next in reference to the letter recipient.

Types of Letters

Three basic types of letters are normally written in response to vacancy announcements:

- Cover letters

- Resume letters

- "T" letters

Cover letters written in response to job vacancy announcements differ from other types of cover letters in one major respect – they respond to the specific requirements outlined in the vacancy announcement. As such, they do much more than merely provide cover for your resume. They focus your qualifications in reference to the needs of the employer. They tell employers that you have the necessary experience and qualifications as stated in the vacancy announcement, as well as reflected in your resume.

Resume letters are letters of application which are not accompanied by a resume. When written in response to a vacancy announcement, a resume letter summarizes your qualifications in reference to the requirements outlined in the vacancy announcement. We examine the special case of resume letters in Chapter 8.

"T" letters are a special type of cover letter which may actually be used like a resume letter – sent in lieu of a resume. They are some of the most powerful job search letters you should include in your writing arsenal. These letters are organized in a two-column "T" format. The writer highlights the employer's requisite qualifications in the first column and then enumerates his or her relevant qualifications in the second column. This "T" format allows the job seeker to target his or her specific accomplishments to the needs of the employer. Such letters clearly communicate to employers that the letter writer either meets or exceeds the requirements for the job. We include examples of these effective letters on pages 133 and 148.

Follow Up Challenge

Job search letters written in response to vacancy announcements may or may not be addressed to a specific name or organization. In many cases an announcement will give the name of the person to whom an application letter and resume should be submitted. This contact name will enable you to include a follow-up statement in your letter. In other cases a classified ad only lists a postal box number or a mailing address minus an organizational or contact name. In these cases you do not know the identity of the organization or its location. Letters responding to such

There is no such thing as a perfect or model cover letter that really works.

anonymous ads will not include follow-up statements. They are least likely to receive a positive response – or any response at all. The letter examples in this chapter include responses to these different types of vacancy announcements.

Remember to Take Action

If an ad or vacancy announcement reveals a contact name, address, or phone number, be sure to include a follow-up statement at the end of your letter. The reason most cover letters in response to vacancy announcements are ineffective has little to do with the contents or quality of the letter. Rather, most letter writers fail to follow up with a phone call.

The follow-up phone call is **the** key to making such cover letters effective. Without the phone call, your letter and resume join an ocean of other similar resumes and letters. The follow-up statement alerts the letter recipient that he or she needs to read your resume and letter because you will be calling to inquire about your candidacy. This statement may also hasten a hiring decision – positive or negative.

If you send cover letters without such follow-up statements, or you fail to follow up with a phone call, don't expect to hear from employers. If you want action on the part of the employer, you must initiate the necessary action to ensure a response.

Again, there is no magic inherent in job search letters or resumes. Your written communication activities must be related to other equally important job search communication activities. There is no such thing as a perfect or model cover letter that really works.

The only thing that really works is you communicating directly with hiring officials. This occurs in the form of telephone or face-to-face interviews. Resumes and letters accompanied by a follow-up telephone call best get hiring officials to take action that gives positive direction to your job search.

Accounting Clerk

3713 Wilson Blvd.
Syracuse, NY 14992

May 2, 20____

SYRACUSE DAILY
Box M1108
Syracuse, NY 14992

I enclose a copy of my resume in reference to your announcement for an Accounting Clerk. With six years of progressive experience in accounting, I would bring to this position

- familiarity with AP/AR, billing, pricing, and cash receipts
- excellent typing (80 wpm) and filing skills
- knowledge of word processing, spreadsheet, and database programs (Word, Excel, Lotus, Access)

While my most recent experience is with the DBC accounting system, I'm also familiar with several other business programs.

I would appreciate an opportunity to interview for this position.

Sincerely,

Martha Ellis

Martha Ellis
ellism@earthone.com

Athletic Director

LAURIE MAYNARD   maynardl@aol.com

819 Switchback Road   Atlanta, GA 33913   291-309-3920

October 3, 20____

John Barnard
ATLANTA CLUB
918 Peachtree Ave.
Atlanta, GA 33919

Dear Mr. Barnard:

As the manager of the premier health club in Atlanta, you know how important it is to maintain a quality facility. And your club is one of the finest in the southeast. I know because I've visited many throughout the state as well as in Florida, South Carolina, Tennessee, and Alabama.

I'm especially interested in the Athletic Director position you advertised in today's <u>Atlanta Constitution</u>. As indicated in the accompanying resume, I have several years of experience as the Assistant Athletic Director at Atlanta Central High School. In addition, during the past two years, I have worked part-time as both an instructor and publicist at the Peachtree Health Club.

I believe I possess the necessary skills to do a first-class job as your Athletic Director. I helped plan, organize, and direct more than eight sports activities involving a student body of over 1,000. In addition, I was instrumental in developing a special athletic program for faculty and parents. I've made numerous presentations and know how to effectively market sports programs.

If you are looking for someone who takes initiative, can manage people, communicates well, knows how to market, and simply loves operating and developing sports programs, let's meet soon to discuss this position. I'll call you on Thursday afternoon to see if you have any questions about my candidacy. I have several ideas on how an Athletic Director with a background in education can best meet your needs.

Sincerely,

Laurie Maynard

Laurie Maynard
maynardl@aol.com

Building Engineer

731 Ocean Breeze Dr.
Miami, FL 31114
February 7, 20____

Terry Barton
KEY MANAGEMENT CO.
7820 Ocean Blvd., Suite 131
Miami, FL 31110

Dear Mr. Barton:

I read with interest your ad in today's <u>Miami Herald</u> for a Building Engineer to handle a 130-unit condo project. I believe I have the necessary experience to do an excellent job. In addition, I am willing to live on the premises.

I have nearly seven years of experience as a Building Engineer. My experience involved:

- working with all aspects of central heating plants
- diagnosing and resolving mechanical, electrical, and plumbing problems
- preparing equipment for inspections
- reporting monthly inspections to the condo association president and presenting an annual inspection report to association members

I pride myself on operating an effective preventive maintenance program which includes timely inspections and routine reporting procedures.

I would appreciate an opportunity to interview for this position. I'm especially interested in sharing with you a model preventive maintenance program I developed in my current job. It enabled the condo association to save over $100,000 a year in unnecessary repairs.

I'll call your office next Monday to see if you have any questions concerning my candidacy. I look forward to meeting you and learning more about the position.

Sincerely,

Samuel Rittenstone

Samuel Rittenstone
rittenstone@mymail.com

Circulation Intern

712 W. Vermont St.
Washington, DC 20132

May 3, 20____

Elliott Stevens
WASHINGTON MONTHLY
1611 Connecticut Ave., NW
Washington, DC 20009

Dear Mr. Stevens:

While visiting the Department of Journalism at George Washington University today, I saw your announcement for a Summer Circulation Intern. I'm enclosing my resume as an application for this position.

I would really love working for the <u>Washington Monthly</u>. It's one of my favorite magazines. It maintains a unique muckraking tradition that is absent in much of today's print journalism. It would be exciting to play a role in increasing the circulation of your magazine.

I know my work experience in journalism is very limited. As a junior majoring in journalism, I've spent most of my time studying (18-hour semester course loads) while participating in some student activities. I'm taking off this summer to gain work experience relevant to my major. My long-term goal is to become an investigative reporter and then a manager of a newspaper or magazine.

While I don't have a great deal to offer you in terms of experience, I am a highly motivated, hard worker who wants to really learn the business from the bottom up. This internship will enable me to learn a great deal about promotion and distribution – areas which I have enjoyed the most in my journalism studies – while also contributing to the promotion of my favorite magazine.

If you give me an opportunity to interview for this position, I promise you will not be disappointed. I'll call you on Friday morning to see if we might be able to meet to discuss the position.

Sincerely,

Tracy Nelson

Tracy Nelson
tracynelson@hotmail.com

Consumer Advocate

ROBBIN BARRETT   barrettr@aol.com

221 Western Avenue   Detroit, MI 47892   919-231-3214

November 5, 20____

Katherine Kerry
Recruitment Director
CONSUMER UNION
29 Temple Place
Boston, MA 02111

Dear Ms. Kerry:

I read with interest your announcement for a Consumer Program Associate in the February issue of Community Jobs. This is an exciting position that should have a major impact on environmental and energy legislation.

As indicated in the enclosed resume, I believe my interests and background are ideally suited to this position. While completing my BA in communication, I promoted awareness of environmental and energy issues as a reporter for our campus newspaper. As a member of the Student Environmental Awareness Group, I helped organize conferences and successfully led demonstrations protesting the construction of a new library on the site of the campus arboretum. My involvement with such activities and issues convinced me to pursue an activist career relating to such public issues.

During the past three years I have been involved in all advocacy phases relating to consumer, environmental, and energy issues:

- Lobbied state and local officials.
- Promoted consumer issues with campus groups and the media.
- Managed a citizen outreach office.
- Developed press materials and promotional strategies.

I have a strong interest and commitment to these issues. I know how to work well with citizen groups, public officials, business groups, and the media.

I appreciate your consideration and look forward to discussing with you how I might best work with your organization. I'll call you next Wednesday to answer any questions you might have about my qualifications.

Sincerely,

Robbin Barrett

Robbin Barrett

Cost Containment Coordinator

DOROTHY HINES   hinesd@earthweb.net

9132 S. Wright Street   Providence, RI 01328   314-367-2874

June 14, 20____

Marilyn Deitz
THE HEALTH GROUP
7134 W. Madison
New Haven, CT 02814

Dear Ms. Deitz:

I read with interest your ad in this month's issue of <u>Healthcare Today</u> for a Cost Containment Coordinator. I am especially interested in this position because it is one of the most important for maintaining the financial viability of healthcare programs.

As indicated in the accompanying resume, I have an LPN and more than five years of experience in collecting, analyzing, and reporting health-care cost and utilization data. I'm also skilled in the use of computer- based data management systems and Lotus 1-2-3.

This position is ideally suited for my background and interests. I've previously worked for both an insurance company and a hospital and thus am very familiar with claims processing. I also played a major role in developing a hospital audit and physician review program at Providence Central Hospital.

Would you have a few minutes to speak with me about this position? I have a few ideas I would like to share with you on alternative ways to organize claims processing. I'll call you on Wednesday to check your schedule.

Sincerely,

Dorothy Hines

Dorothy Hines

Criminal Justice

MARCUS WELLINGTON, Ph.D.   wellingtonm@aol.com

213 Annapolis Road   Annapolis, MD 24212   401-238-3192

January 7, 20____

Cheryl Grant, Personnel Director
Department of Public Safety
   and Correctional Services
6111 Reisterstown Road, Suite 110
Baltimore, MD 21222-3142

Dear Ms. Grant:

I read with interest your vacancy announcement in the Sunday edition of The Baltimore Sun for Director, Division of Parole and Probation. As requested, I enclose a copy of my resume for your consideration.

I bring to this position nearly 10 years of progressive experience in the Maryland criminal justice system. After completing my B.A. in Criminal Justice from the University of Maryland, I worked as a police officer in Baltimore. I was especially fortunate to work alongside one of the city's leaders in correctional administration, R. Lance Donovan, who encouraged me to pursue a master's degree in public administration with a specialty in correctional administration.

Since completing my graduate work 8 years ago, I've had a wonderful career in correctional administration. My work in the fields of parole and probation have convinced me of the importance of developing new approaches to correctional administration. During the past three years I've been involved in developing a model probation program that has reduced recidivism rates by nearly 30% within a two-year period. I'm excited about the opportunity this position would afford me to use my experience to further improve Maryland's parole and probation programs.

I would appreciate an opportunity to meet with you to discuss how my interests and qualifications can best meet your needs. I'll call your office next Wednesday to see if we might be able to meet at a mutually convenient time. I have several ideas I would like to share with you about how I might approach this position.

Sincerely,

Marcus Wellington

Marcus Wellington

Director, Business Operations
(Health Care)

STEVEN O'BRIEN   obriens@planetone.com

7891 Donner Lane   Orlando, FL 35421   913/371-3981

July 5, 20____

Ms. Sharon Campbell
Director, Operations Support
DENVER GENERAL HOSPITAL
2033 Spring Road
Denver, CA 80023

Dear Ms. Campbell:

Your ad in yesterday's <u>Denver Post</u> for a Director of Business Operations attracted my attention for several reasons. I bring to this job:

- 8 years of experience in healthcare finance with a 600+ bed acute care facility
- 5 years of progressively responsible reimbursement experience
- 3 years of management level experience in healthcare billing and collections
- familiarity with major computerized accounting and spread-sheet systems
- a solid record of accomplishment – increased collections by 47% and reduced accounting costs by 36% during the past two years as Assistant Director of Business Operations at Orlando General Hospital

I'm especially interested in moving to Denver where I spent my undergraduate years at the University of Denver. With family there, I already feel part of the community.

I enclose a copy of my resume as well as an article I recently completed on health-care finance for your reference. The article summarizes much of my philosophy on healthcare finance approaches.

I'll call your office next Thursday afternoon to answer any questions you might have about my candidacy. I also have a few questions about the position.

Sincerely,

Steven O'Brien

Steven O'Brien

Dispatcher

882 Forest Lane
Cleveland, OH 43210

March 1, 20____

P.O. Box 82
Cleveland, OH 43207

Here's my resume in response to your ad in today's Cleveland Plain Dealer for an evening dispatcher. I'm very familiar – nine years experience – with all aspects of trucking, warehouse, and communication operations. I worked as a driver for three years, a stevedore for two years, and an assistant warehouse manager for one year. During the past three years I've been an evening dispatcher with Bluebird Trucking. I have computer experience and I'm noted for working well with others in stressful settings.

I would appreciate more information on this position and your organization, as well as an opportunity to interview for this position. Please give me a call if you need any additional information. You will find I have a pleasant telephone manner which is essential for a good dispatcher.

Sincerely,

Jack Diamond

Jack Diamond
diamondj@earthnet.com

Dispute Resolution Intake Coordinator

2908 Trail Drive
Atlanta, GA 32119
September 29, 20____

Barbara Haynes
Department of Dispute Resolution
SUPREME COURT OF GEORGIA
100 N. Eighth Street, 2nd Floor
Atlanta, GA 32109

Dear Ms. Haynes:

I am enclosing my resume and the state application form you requested in response to the announcement for a Dispute Resolution Intake Coordinator for DeKalb County which appeared in last Sunday's Atlanta Constitution. I believe my interests and experience nicely coincide with the requirements for this position.

I have a master's degree in Public Administration with a specialty in state court administration. As an undergraduate majoring in Criminal Justice, I worked two summers as a paralegal. As part of my graduate work, I interned with the state Office of Court Administration. There I became very familiar with the problems of an overloaded court system. Indeed, I was fortunate to work closely with a talented group of professionals who developed a pilot dispute referral and mediation program. I was especially delighted to learn their efforts were translated into what may well become a model program for other state court systems.

But what can I bring to this position that others may not? I am very familiar with your program. I'm experienced in

- screening and assessing court cases for possible mediation
- conducting group orientations and individual assessments
- developing and maintaining lists of mediators
- evaluating program effectiveness
- developing criteria for case referral

I have worked closely with court administrators and community leaders in publicizing alternative programs for dispute resolution. I also have grantsmanship skills which should prove useful for this program.

I would appreciate an opportunity to interview for this position. I will call you Thursday morning to check on my application and to see if you have any questions concerning my background and skills.

Sincerely,

Kevin Anderson

Kevin Anderson
kanderson@ace.com

Editor

MALISSA GROVES   grovesm@terros.net

819 Elm Grove Circle   Boston, MA 02331   415-367-9220

August 17, 20____

Janet Akers
NATIONAL ASSOCIATION
   OF REALTORS
777 14th Street, NW
Washington, DC 20005

Dear Ms. Akers:

I'm submitting my resume and three writing samples in response to your announcement in today's Washington Post for an editor of the biweekly newspaper, Realtor News. I'm especially interested in this position because of my extensive reporting and editorial work on real estate. I would bring to this position

- six years of progressively responsible experience in reporting, writing, and editing
- extensive knowledge of the real estate industry
- an ability to meet tight deadlines
- an eagerness to work closely with fellow professionals

As indicated in my sample clippings, I've written and edited several lead articles on the real estate industry. I am also completing a book on today's changing real estate market which will be published next year. I believe I will bring to this position a solid record of writing and editing accomplishments.

I would appreciate an opportunity to discuss how my interests and qualifications can best meet your needs. I will call you on Tuesday afternoon to answer any questions you might have about my candidacy.

Sincerely,

Malissa Groves

Malissa Groves

Education

714 W. 42nd St.
Bremerton, WA 98213
October 21, 20___

Bruce Davidson
Department of Personnel/
    Human Resources
WALTON MIDDLE SCHOOL DISTRICT
401 McIntire Road
Seattle, WA 98111

Dear Mr. Davidson:

I enclose my resume in response to your announcement in today's <u>Seattle Times</u> for Principal of Walton Middle School. I would bring to this position

- 18 years of progressive experience in education, as both a classroom teacher and administrator

- a demonstrated record of teaching excellence, including teaching awards

- the ability to supervise teachers and classified staff

- a willingness to work closely with parents, teachers, and community leaders

I am currently completing my Ph.D. in educational administration with a specialty in elementary education.

Please let me know if you need any additional information. I will call you Thursday morning to see if you have any questions about my candidacy. I would appreciate an opportunity to interview for this position.

Sincerely,

Tina Stewart

Tina Stewart
stewartt@atlas.com

Electronic Technician

4421 Sherman Avenue
Gainesville, FL 33412
May 29, 20____

James Thurber
ELECTRODYNE, INC.
8213 Bertram Road
Gainesville, FL 33410

Dear Mr. Thurber:

I enclose my resume in response to your announcement for a Field Service Technician or Technician Supervisor that appeared in today's Gainesville Sentinel. Based on the description, the positions appear ideally suited to my interests and skills.

I have a two-year degree in electronics from the Electronics Institute. During the past three years I have worked as both a Field Service Technician and Technician Supervisor for Gainesville Cablevision. These jobs required excellent communication skills and trouble-shooting capabilities. My supervisor judged my performance to be "outstanding." Indeed, I was promoted to Technician Supervisor within 18 months.

Your ad requested salary history. When I started with Gainesville Cablevision, I made $24,500 a year. This year I am making $33,350 a year. I would expect this to increase to $34,650 by next year.

I would appreciate an opportunity to meet with you to discuss how my experience can best meet your needs. I will call you Wednesday afternoon to answer any questions you may have about my candidacy.

Sincerely,

Debra White

Debra White
whited@aol.com

Employment Counselor

766 Oro Rio Drive
San Luis Obispo, CA 98734
February 21, 20____

Bernard Tompkins, Manager
SUNSHINE TEMPORARY SERVICES
7638 Costa del Sur
Santa Barbara, CA 98763

Dear Mr. Tompkins:

For the past three years I have been an employment counselor with Solutions
for Hire Temporary Services in San Luis Obispo. I like the opportunity to work
with people – both the temporaries and the employers – and enjoy helping
them solve their employment problems.

I am responding to your advertisement for an employment counselor that
appeared in today's edition of the <u>Santa Barbara Sun Times</u>. I will be moving
to Santa Barbara in two weeks. Since I really enjoy working as an employment
counselor, your position appears to be ideally suited to my interests, skills, and
accomplishments.

I enclose my resume which will give you an overview of my background. Two
of my accomplishments most pertinent to your advertised opening are:

- Started a new division in our office called "helping hands." This
  division, which provides unskilled workers to factories, has proven
  so successful, our company has adopted the program in its branch
  offices nationwide.

- Initiated a temp-employer feedback program that has resulted in
  a 23% increase in business because of greater employer satisfaction with the temporary help we provide.

I look forward to meeting with you and having the opportunity to talk with
you further regarding your needs and what I could bring to Sunshine Temporary Services.

Sincerely,

Jake Weber

Jake Weber
<u>weberj@aol.com</u>

Environmental Engineer

717 N. Abbott St.
Amherst, MA 02432

March 22, 20____

Marilyn Reed
RTC TECHNOLOGY
188 Stevens Drive
St. Louis, MO 63211

Dear Ms. Reed:

I noticed with interest your announcement for an environmental engineer specializing in hazardous waste processing which was posted in the career office of the engineering department at the University of Massachusetts. I'm completing my master's degree and will be available for full-time employment beginning in June.

I enclose my resume for your reference. During the past two years I have had an opportunity to both study and work in the environmental engineering field. My course work has focused on the engineering aspects of hazardous waste processing. During the past two summers I interned with one of the nation's largest environmental engineering firms, BTS Technology.

I would appreciate an opportunity to interview for this position. I will call your office Friday morning to see if you have any questions concerning my candidacy.

Sincerely,

Aaron Trisler

Aaron Trisler
trislera@rollis.com

Executive Secretary

SHARON EVERS   everss@erols.com

1324 Thomas Circle   Mobile, AL 35214   208-378-1392

November 5, 20____

Julian Woods
C.H. JAMISON ASSOCIATES
8714 Norton Avenue
Mobile, AL 35211

Dear Mr. Woods:

The Executive Secretary position you advertised in today's <u>Mobile Times</u> especially interests me. As the enclosed resume indicates, I have over seven years of secretarial experience. During the past three years I've served as executive secretary to a financial investment firm of 85 employees. I regularly use Word and Excel and can quickly master other software programs as well as train employees.

You will also find that I am a dependable, loyal, and enthusiastic employee who works well under the pressure of deadlines. My previous employers gave me high marks for my administrative abilities in organizing office routines, handling travel schedules, communicating with departments, and organizing and planning meetings. I very much enjoy being Executive Secretary in a work environment that supports initiative and creativity.

I would appreciate an opportunity to interview for this position. I will call you Wednesday morning to see if you have any questions concerning my application.

Thank you for your consideration.

Sincerely,

Sharon Evers

Sharon Evers

Financial Analyst

ROBIN ANSLER   anslerr@citynet.com

1061 Wilson Blvd.   Arlington, VA 23122   703-881-8291

January 30, 20____

Albert Jones
WORLDCOM
12220 Sunrise Valley Drive
Reston, VA 22098

Dear Mr. Jones:

I know the importance of maintaining a sound financial analysis in the communication business. That's why I was attracted to your ad in the <u>Washington Times</u> for a Financial Analyst.

During the past four years I've worked in a similar position at AT&T. We developed one of the most innovative financial reporting programs in the industry. It helped increase the profitability of WorldCom's Voice Products by 22%.

I know your products and services well. Indeed, as AT&T's major competitor for offshore customers, WorldCom has an excellent reputation for quality. It's the type of organization I find most attractive for the financial skills I possess. I believe we would work well together.

As indicated in the accompanying resume and in reference to the qualifications outlined in your ad, I have a BA in Accounting and an MBA in Finance. I regularly work with Lotus, Peoplesoft, and Excel and exhibit strong oral and written communication skills.

I'll call your office Tuesday morning to see if you have any questions about my candidacy. I would appreciate an opportunity to discuss with you how my skills and experience can best meet WorldCom's needs.

Sincerely,

Robin Ansler

Robin Ansler

Grants Specialist

ANDREW CLARK
253 North Shore Dr.
Chicago, IL 60011
312-381-0812
clarka@earthweb.com

February 18, 20____

Elizabeth Marlo, Ph.D.
Office of Faculty Development
UNIVERSITY OF ILLINOIS
One University Plaza
Chicago, IL 60015

Dear Dr. Marlo:

Can the University of Illinois use a Grants Specialist who can increase grants by 15% in a single year? That's what I've accomplished this past year as a Grants Specialist at Roosevelt University. This 15% increase translated into $4.2 million in additional grants awarded to the university. The resulting overhead increases enabled the university to create two new positions in Faculty Development.

I read with interest your announcement for a Grants Specialist in <u>The Chronicle of Higher Education</u>. As indicated in the accompanying resume, I have over eight years of grantsmanship experience in higher education. I've been involved in all phases of grants management, from developing and administering contracts, grants, and cooperative agreements with government agencies, corporations, and foundations to assisting faculty in developing proposal skills.

I would appreciate an opportunity to discuss how my qualifications can best meet your needs. I am especially interested in sharing with you a grantsmanship training program I developed at Roosevelt University for improving the capabilities of faculty to generate winning proposals.

I'll call your office Monday afternoon to answer any questions you may have about my qualifications. I look forward to meeting you.

Sincerely,

Andrew Clark

Andrew Clark

Graphic Artist

DEBRA SUMMERS   summersdeb@aol.com

781 Humphrey Blvd.   Minneapolis, MN 53821   812-928-0132

July 19, 20____

Sandra Delray
OLLEN GRAPHICS
182 Thompson Avenue
Suite 914
Minneapolis, MN 53824

Dear Ms. Delray:

The Graphic Artist position you advertised in today's <u>Minneapolis Times</u> fits me perfectly. I have the necessary motivation, skills, and experience to excel in this position.

I enclose a copy of my resume as well as a few samples of my work for your reference. These reflect a strong background in computerized graphic design. As indicated in your ad, you need someone who has expertise with Word, Excel, and PageMaker and who can do design and layout. I've worked with all of these programs and do design and layout up on a daily basis.

I'll call you Wednesday morning to see if we might get together soon to discuss this position. I'm interested in learning more about your studio.

Sincerely,

Debra Summers

Debra Summers

Health Education Evaluator

891 Wheeler Road
Charlotte, NC 34317
December 1, 20____

Ronald Rittenhouse, Director
Office of Human Resources
HEALTH RESOURCES, INC.
716 Sunnyside Avenue
Charlotte, NC 34317

Dear Mr. Rittenhouse:

I read with interest your ad in today's edition of the <u>Charlotte Times</u> for a
Health Education Evaluator. As indicated in the accompanying resume and list of
publications, I believe my background is ideally suited for this position.

I completed my MPH seven years ago at the University of North Carolina in
Chapel Hill. Since then I have worked with the North Carolina Department of
Health as a program analyst. After leaving the Department three years ago, I
completed additional graduate work and did part-time evaluation research work
with several health care firms. My reports have been well received by employers
who regularly use me for part-time contract work.

I am interested in re-entering the health field on a full-time basis. As a former
state employee involved in major health care policy issues and skilled in evaluation
research, I believe I would bring to this position a unique blend of experience and
skills that would prove invaluable to your organization. I am very familiar with the
programs outlined in your ad and have expertise in the three program areas you
mention – community program development, minority health education program
development and implementation, and women's health issues.

We should meet to discuss how my background best fits into your hiring
needs. I will call your office on Thursday morning to see if you have any questions
as well as ask a few of my own. For example, are you familiar with the new NHC
model which may soon be implemented at the state level? This is an area I'm very
familiar with and which I believe has extremely important implications for minority health education programs and the contractors who deliver services to such
programs.

Sincerely,

John Zigler

John Zigler
jzigpler@yahoo.com

Healthcare – Clinical Data Analyst

STEPHANIE OLSON
382 Winter Green Dr.
Philadelphia, PA 17923
216-378-2981
olsons@earthone.net

October 9, 20___

David Maris
KAISER PERMANENTE
P.O. Box 9884
Philadelphia, PA 17929

Dear Mr. Maris:

Your ad in today's <u>Philadelphia Inquirer</u> for a Clinical Data Analyst caught my attention. I have a master's degree in Public Health and four years experience as an analyst providing technical support for quality assurance. I especially enjoy working with statistical analysis.

As indicated in the accompanying resume, my experience includes the skills you require – developed and maintained computerized databases for peer review, quality screen, and clinical studies. In addition, I am very familiar with personal computers and database management in healthcare. This includes knowledge and experience in Paradox, DB Graphics, RBase, and Access.

I would appreciate an opportunity to interview for this position. I will call your office on Tuesday afternoon to see if you have any questions about my candidacy.

Sincerely,

Stephanie Olson

Stephanie Olson

Hotel – Guest Services Manager

WAYNE STEINBERG   steinbergw@erols.com

5491 Mountain Drive   Sacramento, CA 95421   219-729-2912

July 8, 20____

Martha Albertson
Personnel Department
HOLIDAY INN NATIONAL
319 Granite Stone Dr.
San Diego, CA 92351

Dear Ms. Albertson:

Your ad in today's <u>San Diego Times</u> for a Guest Services Manager caught my attention. Therefore, I'm submitting my resume as an application for this position.

I believe I have the necessary experience to manage guest services for your 300-room hotel. My experience includes:

- three years supervisory experience – both AM and PM shifts
- strong rate management skills
- cost controls of payroll and expenses
- training guest relations personnel

I also have received extensive training in night audit.

I would appreciate an opportunity to interview for this position. I'll call your office on Tuesday afternoon to answer any questions you may have about my candidacy.

Sincerely,

Wayne Steinberg

Wayne Steinberg

Human Resources Analyst

JANET ENGLE
241 Marlboro Lane
Raleigh, NC 27210
717-894-2281
englej@earthnet.com

March 11, 20___

Gloria Manns
CHARLOTTE-MECKLENBURG
      SCHOOLS
P.O. Box 30154
Charlotte, NC 28241

Dear Ms. Manns:

Your recent ad in <u>School Administrator</u> for a Human Resources Analyst
interests me for several reasons. I have the necessary qualifications you
outlined for this position. I'm very attracted to the Charlotte area. And I
believe this is a position in which I would excel.

I would bring to this position several important qualifications and experiences acquired during my 15 years of work in education:

- master's degree in Psychology
- experience in job evaluation, benefits administration, compensation analysis, performance design, and quality intervention
- microcomputer proficiency
- knowledge of performance measurement and design models

I would appreciate an opportunity to interview for this position. Please
expect a call from me Thursday afternoon. I have a few questions concerning this position. Perhaps you also may have questions about my
candidacy.

Sincerely,

Janet Engle

Janet Engle

Information Services Librarian

JULIE STROOMER   stroomerj@erols.com

179 W. 27th Street   San Francisco, CA 94131   419-384-2093

August 25, 20___

Betsy Kramer
AMERICAN SCHOOL BOARDS
   ASSOCIATION
2792 Hillcrest Dr.
San Francisco, CA 94123

Dear Ms. Kramer:

My 10 years of experience as an Information Services Librarian appears to
be ideally suited for the position you advertised in this month's issue of
America's Schools. You need someone who can

- oversee the activities of your organization's information services,
  resource center, and clearinghouses
- provide staff and constituents with information when needed
- manage day-to-day communications operations
- supervise a group of five employees
- demonstrate strong oral and written communication skills

As indicated on my enclosed resume, I acquired this experience over a 15-
year period as the Information Services Librarian for U.S. Department of
Interior's regional library service and as a high school librarian.

I also meet the qualifications you specify for this position. I have a master's
degree in Library Science with an emphasis on managing library information
systems. Since I have worked closely with secondary and elementary schools,
I am very knowledgeable about education and school governance issues as
well as information and reference sources in education. During the past five
years I supervised eight employees.

I would appreciate an opportunity to meet with you to discuss how my
experience and qualifications can best meet your needs. I have additional
skills which you might find useful for this particular position. I will call you
on Wednesday morning to answer any questions you may have concerning
my candidacy.

Sincerely,

Julie Stroomer

Julie Stroomer

Information Systems Specialist

231 Westview Terrace
Benton Harbor, MI 48270

February 27, 20____

Eric Nelson
NCCR, INC.
1900 North Echos Road
Benton Harbor, MI 48271

Dear Mr. Nelson:

I read with interest your ad in the <u>Benton Harbor Times</u> for an Information Systems Specialist. As the accompanying resume indicates, I have the requisite skills and experience you outlined for this position. My 12 years with the U.S. Navy has prepared me well in the use of numerous computer systems and languages.

You may also be interested in several additional skills I would bring to this position:

- designed, coded, and tested network application software
- proficient in several high level computer languages ("C," etc.) and operating systems (UNIX, DOS) and window systems (X-Windows)
- planned systems management for communications network
- conducted research and development work on systems management and network simulation

I would appreciate an opportunity to interview for this position. I will call you on Thursday morning to answer any questions you may have concerning my candidacy.

Sincerely,

Debra Winston

Debra Winston
winstond@aol.com

Insurance Casualty Claim Adjuster

1103 Wilson Blvd.
Buffalo, NY 14830

March 8, 20____

Sharon Drews
SILVAN CORPORATION
913 Benton Road
Buffalo, NY 14832

Dear Ms. Drews:

I enclose my resume in response to your ad in today's <u>Buffalo Evening Star</u> for a Casualty Claims Adjustor. This position is ideally suited for my skills and experience.

I have a bachelor's degree in Business and five years of progressively responsible experience handling worker's compensation and general liability claims. During the past two years I have been responsible for developing an innovative casualty claims system for the American Insurance Company. I believe my work with this system may be of interest to Silvan Corporation.

Please let me know if you need any additional information to complete my application. I'll call you on Tuesday afternoon to answer any questions you may have about my candidacy.

Sincerely,

Beth Clarion

Beth Clarion
<u>clarionb@earthlink.com</u>

Interior Design/Sales

1093 Martin Falls Rd.
Newark, NJ 07194

April 4, 20____

Box M118
NEWARK DAILY
Newark, NJ 07192

Are you looking for someone who can increase your sales by 50% within six months? If so, you need not look further. During my first six months as a sales associate for C. Irwin Interiors, I increased sales of furniture and furnishings/accessories by 50%. More importantly, this translated into $650,000 in additional commercial business. Since then, I've remained one of the company's top performers.

I enclose my resume in response to your ad in today's newspaper for an Interior Design/Sales position. We should meet soon to discuss how my experience and approach to interior design sales can best benefit your firm.

I look forward to hearing from you.

Sincerely,

Brenda Faris

Brenda Faris
farisb@earthland.com

International Development

LYNNE GARDNER   gardnerl@planet.net

8172 Western Avenue   Cedar Rapids, IA 54019   412-/382-1333

August 17, 20____

Morris Edelson
Recruitment Committee
ICRW INTERNATIONAL
28 W. 32nd Street
New York, NY 10031

Dear Mr. Edelson:

Your ad in this week's issue of the <u>International Employment Gazette</u> for a social scientist to work on international development issues struck my attention for several reasons:

- I have over 12 years experience in international development – seven involving residence abroad as a Peace Corps Volunteer, student, and contractor/consultant.

- I have the policy-relevant experience you require – completed my Ph.D. dissertation on women in development issues, as well as conducted three consulting projects on family planning policy in Asia and Africa.

- I have contract administration and supervisory experience at the field level.

- I am prepared to relocate abroad for a two- to three-year project period.

I would very much appreciate an opportunity to interview for this position. I will call your office on Friday morning to answer any questions you may have about my previous work and how my experience and skills could best ensure a successful project for ICRW International.

Sincerely,

Lynne Gardner

Lynne Gardner

Laboratory Technician

116 Grandview Road
Dallas, TX 78217

May 23, 20____

Jed Jamison
Human Resources
LATIMORE LABORATORIES
P.O. Box 138
Dallas, TX 78213

Dear Mr. Jamison:

I enclose my resume in response to your ad in today's <u>Dallas Star</u> for a Laboratory Technician. My educational background, knowledge, and experience appear to perfectly match your stated requirements.

I have a B.S. in Biology from North Texas State University. During the past three years I have been employed by Douglas Laboratories in its DNA products laboratory. I regularly work with DNA sequencing, plasmid purification, and recombinant techniques.

You requested that salary requirements accompany the resume. My requirements are flexible at this time. My current salary is $36,500 – about average for an entry-level position plus three years experience in this field. While I would expect a salary commensurate with my level of experience, I need to know more about the position and your organization before I can give you a figure.

I would appreciate an opportunity to discuss this position with you. I will call you on Tuesday afternoon to answer any questions you may have about my candidacy.

Sincerely,

Gerry Gray

Gerry Gray
ggray@hotmail.com

Landscape Architect

MARILYN JACOBS
4215 Florida Ave.
Orlando, FL 31483
Tel. 309-318-2851
Fax 309-318-2777
jacobsm@atlas.com

April 3, 20____

James O'Brien
NEW MARKET FARMS
131 Market St.
Orlando, FL 31486

Dear Mr. O'Brien:

As requested in your announcement in today's <u>Orlando Times</u> for a Landscape Architect, I'm enclosing my resume and a sample of my work. I have a BSLA and two years of design experience primarily working on large commercial projects.

I'm especially interested in this position because your firm has an excellent reputation for doing some of the most creative and innovative commercial landscape work in the Orlando area. It's the type of firm I would be pleased to join.

I would appreciate an opportunity to interview for this position as well as share with you more examples of my work. I am noted for combining arid Southern California styles with more tropical Florida styles. My work has been well received by my present employer who regularly receives praise from satisfied clients.

I will call you on Wednesday morning to answer any questions you may have about my application.

Sincerely,

Marilyn Jacobs

Marilyn Jacobs

Legal Secretary

7172 Whispering Willow Rd.
Columbus, OH 45183

June 4, 20____

Thomas Pickering
DIAMOND, ESTER, AND GRACE
718 Jason Avenue
Columbus, OH 45183

Dear Mr. Pickering:

I'm responding to your ad that appeared in Sunday's <u>Columbus Dispatch</u> for a legal secretary. I have seven years of experience working for a mid-size law firm specializing in patent law. I would bring to this position the following experience and skills:

- ability to both type and take shorthand at 80+ wpm
- familiarity with the latest versions of Word and WordPerfect
- excellent spelling and grammar skills
- energy, enthusiasm, and the ability to work on my own

I am used to working under deadlines and I am willing to work overtime to get the job done.

Your ad also requested information on salary requirements. My current salary is $35,500 per year with full benefits. Given my level of experience as well as current salary ranges for legal secretaries in patent law, I would expect to be offered this position in the $37,000 to $39,000 range, depending on the requirements of the job.

Please let me know if you need any additional information. I'll call you on Tuesday afternoon to answer any questions you may have concerning my candidacy.

Sincerely,

Margo Redding

Margo Redding
<u>redding@aol.com</u>

Legislative Assistant

MICHAEL SHIELDS
313 Wyoming Avenue
Washington, DC 20018
202-718-8291
shieldsm@aol.com

June 19, 20____

Margaret Ballantine
FIELD, STERLING, AND JAMES
1191 Connecticut Ave., NW
Suite 918
Washington, DC 20036

Dear Ms. Ballantine:

After working on Capitol Hill for three years as a Legislative Assistant
to two members of Congress, I'm interested in doing similar work with a
government relations firm. That's why your ad in today's <u>Washington Post</u>
caught my attention.

The accompanying resume summarizes my experience on Capitol Hill.
As a Legislative Assistant, I specialized in tax and health issues, which are
the policy areas you mentioned in your ad. I've worked closely with the
relevant congressional committee staffs, government agencies, and
representatives of industry concerned with these two issues. I believe you
will find I have the necessary knowledge and contacts to become a productive member of your team.

Your ad also mentioned MacIntosh experience. I am familiar with
both MacIntosh and IBM systems. I also am familiar with PageMaker and
Ventura desktop publishing systems.

I'll call your office on Thursday morning to answer any questions you
may have about my candidacy.

I look forward to sharing my legislative experience on tax and health
issues with you in the very near future.

Sincerely,

Michael Shields

Michael Shields

Management/Store

3801 Walnut Street
Los Angeles, CA 91080

September 11, 20____

Jennifer Strong
THE GREEN BEAN CO.
241 Greenbrier Road
Los Angeles, CA 91093

Dear Ms. Strong:

I was delighted to learn in today's <u>Milwaukee Journal</u> that you will be opening three branch stores in the Milwaukee area. You have wonderful products which I regularly purchase through your mail order catalog.

But now to discover you are looking for managers of these stores is even more exciting. I want to throw my hat in the ring and let you know why you should interview me for one of these positions.

I enclose my resume for your reference. Please note that I have three years of management experience with Healthy Harvest Heaven. I served as assistant manager until the store closed in March of last year. Unfortunately, the owners decided to close the business and move to Florida. It was a very successful store that left many disappointed customers who will undoubtedly turn to your stores in the very near future.

I believe my management experience and enthusiasm for your products make a winning combination. I'll call you Monday, September 19, to answer any questions you may have about my candidacy.

Sincerely,

Linda Perry

Linda Perry
<u>lindaperry@aol.com</u>

Management/Store Manager

ALICE WALKER
192 West Norton Ave.
Pittsburgh, PA 18291
719-381-9471
alicewalker@erols.com

January 6, 20____

Albert Black
Personnel Department
THE SOUTHLAND CORPORATION
9103 McNeil Street
Philadelphia, PA 17891

Dear Mr. Black:

I read with interest your ad in today's <u>Pittsburgh Times</u> for an experienced Store Manager with good interpersonal skills and three years previous management experience.

As indicated in the accompanying resume, I have the exact skills and experience you require. During the past seven years I have

- managed both a restaurant and retail video store – I know how important good customer relations are to the success of a business!

- supervised up to 12 employees

- made tough hiring and firing decisions

- experienced both the failure and success of two businesses – the restaurant was a victim of arson, but the video store was a phenomenal success – increasing annual rentals/sales by 40%

We should talk soon about this position. I'll call you on Friday morning to answer any questions you may have about my candidacy.

Sincerely,

Alice Walker

Alice Walker

Management Consultant

125 Jordan Street
New York, NY 10027

September 21, 20____

Donald West
MANAGEMENT INTERNATIONAL
742 West 29th Street
New York, NY 10013

Dear Mr. West:

Your ad in this week's issue of the <u>Employment News Weekly</u> for a Management Consultant coincides nicely with my interests and experience. I am very interested in this position and thus am submitting my resume for your consideration.

The ad states you are seeking an experienced manufacturing professional to assist in project work in North America and Europe. I would bring to this position the following relevant experience:

- 10 years operations management experience with competence in World-Class Manufacturing Systems (Total Quality Methods and Team-Based Employee Work Systems)

- 5 years management consulting work in six Western European and three Eastern European countries – fluent in German

In addition, I have been frequently cited by clients for my exceptional planning, communication, and interpersonal skills as well as demonstrated poise, discipline, and maturity.

My salary requirements are in the $70-$80K range, depending on the nature of responsibilities assigned to this position.

I will call you next Thursday afternoon to answer any questions you may have concerning my candidacy.

Sincerely,

Martin Goodman

Martin Goodman
<u>mgoodman@planet2.com</u>

Management/Trainee

GERALD DALTON   daltong@earthnet.com

818 Canyon Road   Riverside, CA 91483   819-290-1982

July 19, 20___

Marc Kaiser
RENT-A-CENTER
9128 Thompson Road
Los Angeles, CA 91589

Dear Mr. Kaiser:

In response to your ad in today's <u>Los Angeles Times</u>, I am enclosing my resume in application for the management opportunities you outlined. I understand you are willing to train individuals for these positions.

My background appears to be ideally suited for this opportunity. I have a bachelor's degree in Accounting. I previously acquired management experience while working in a restaurant and managing a small retail furniture store. From both experiences I learned the importance of maintaining excellent customer relations and operating an efficient collections system – two skill areas you mentioned as important to the management opportunities.

Please expect to hear from me Friday morning. I will call your office to answer any questions you may have about my candidacy.

Sincerely,

Gerald Dalton

Gerald Dalton

Management/Trainee

8004 Elk Grove Dr.
Columbia, SC 32812

November 5, 20____

Box 918
COLUMBIA DISPATCH
Columbia, SC 32812

I read with interest this brief ad that appeared in last Sunday's edition of the Columbia Dispatch:

> MANAGEMENT - Will train aggressive individuals to top level management and six figure income. Rapid advancement to $55K.

Of course, like many others who contact you, I'm interested. I am aggressive but not to the point of being overbearing.

The enclosed resume summarizes my management experience. I have a strong pattern of management success, regardless of whom I work for or the type of organization, product, or service involved.

If I am the type of person you think would be a valuable addition to your operations, then let's talk soon about how we might best work together.

Sincerely,

Martin Throel

Martin Throel
throelm@aol.com

Management/Trainee

334 Winthrop Street
Oak Lawn, IL 60331

July 21, 20____

Box 183
CHICAGO TRIBUNE
183 Michigan Avenue
Chicago, IL 60001

I read with interest your ad in today's <u>Chicago Tribune</u> for college grads interested in a management career with a national company.

As my accompanying resume indicates, I graduated from the University of Illinois in June. I majored in political science and minored in accounting.

I am interested in pursuing a long-term management career with a major national company. While working my way through college, I initially became a waiter and was later promoted to assistant manager of a restaurant. I very much enjoyed my management experience, especially supervising employees and maintaining accurate accounts. I believe this experience as well as my undergraduate studies have prepared me well for a career in management.

I would appreciate an opportunity to interview for this position. I believe you will find I have the necessary prerequisites to excel as a management trainee.

Sincerely,

Gary Turner

Gary Turner
<u>turnerg@aol.com</u>

Management Trainer
(special "T" letter format)

579 Tilman Drive
Pittsburgh, PA 19999
February 14, 20____

Stephanie Ableson
Director of Training
ASTR TRAINING LTD.
172 Wellstone Avenue
Syracuse, NY 18888

Dear Ms. Ableson:

I noticed with interest your ad in *Training Resources* for an experienced
Management Trainer. I would bring to this position these qualifications:

Your Needs	My Qualifications
■ Five years training experience.	■ Seven years of progressive experience as a management trainer in a variety of organizational settings.
■ Strong writing and presentation skills.	■ Annually produce 6-8 training manuals and conduct more than 30 three-day training sessions on a variety of supervisory skills for entry- to senior-level managers.
■ Ability to supervise a group of training professionals	■ Annually supervise 7 trainers who conduct more than 300 programs in 18 U.S. and European locations.

The enclosed resume further summarizes my qualifications. I would
appreciate an opportunity to speak with you about this position. I'll
call your office next Thursday morning to answer any questions you
may have about my candidacy.

Sincerely,

Michael Morris

Michael Morris
morrism@planetnow.net

Manager/Retail Store

2761 Morrow Road
Rushing Falls, NY 10029

August 3, 20____

Janice Jackson
President
VILLAGE STORES
736 Main Street
Rushing Falls, NY 10026

Dear Ms. Jackson:

I read in today's <u>Post</u> of your opening for a manager with experience in women's retailing. I have 15 years experience in retailing of women's clothing – 8 of those in management.

As my enclosed resume indicates, I have been acting manager of Chic Street for the past eight months. The manager of Chic Street will be returning next month following a leave of absence. I believe my management experience and retailing skills would be an asset at Village Stores.

Under my management at Chic Street we were able to:

- increase sales by 23%

- decrease employee turnover by 20%

- eliminate overtime

I am anxious to meet with you to discuss how we might be able to utilize my skills to increase the bottom line at the Village Stores.

Sincerely,

Marilyn Chaffe

Marilyn Chaffe
marilynchaffe@erols.com

Market Analyst

918 Western Blvd.
Kansas City, KS 47831

March 21, 20_____

Martin Jamison
HEALTHCARE ASSOCIATES
9981 Jefferson Highway
Suite 903
Las Vegas, NV 89312

Dear Mr. Jamison:

I just received this month's issue of <u>Healthcare News</u> and noticed your ad for a Market Analyst with consulting experience.

I believe I have the skills and experience you need. In addition to a master's degree in Public Health, I have four years experience as a Market Analyst in the healthcare field. During this time I have conducted over 10 major research projects which involved gathering and analyzing data, writing reports, and presenting findings to funding agencies. I always meet my deadlines and produce first-class products which are well received by sponsors. I am knowledge-able in the use of the two computer programs you mentioned in your ad – Access and Excel.

I would be happy to send you a sample of my work, especially a recent report I completed on the comparative costs of alternative healthcare markets for the U.S. Department of Health and Human Services.

I'll call you next Thursday afternoon to answer any questions you may have about my candidacy.

Sincerely,

George Barton

George Barton
georgebar@citynet.com

Marketing/Art

BEVERLY SIMON   simonb@planetnow.net

29 Little Run Road   Boston, MA 02193   918-382-4510

December 29, 20____

Kerry Klein
INTERNATIONAL ART EXPRESS
792 New England Avenue
Boston, MA 02193

Dear Mr. Klein:

What a wonderful position for someone with an art and marketing background! Your ad in today's <u>Boston Globe</u> for a self-starter to market your Art Leasing programs really caught my attention and immediately sent me to my word processor. It appears perfectly tailored to my interests, skills, and experience. It's as if I had written it for myself.

We really should meet to discuss how I would handle this position. I believe it is the perfect fit for me since the position combines my two loves – art and marketing.

Indeed, I have prepared well for this position. I have a bachelor's degree in Art History and a master's degree in Marketing. In addition, I have worked in two art galleries as the person in charge of sales and marketing. In both cases I was successful in increasing sales by 30% over an 18-month period. Most of this increase was due to my innovative and aggressive approach to the corporate market. I also introduced a successful corporate leasing program which now constitutes 35% of these galleries' revenues.

I will call your office on Friday morning to answer any questions you may have about my candidacy.

Sincerely,

Beverly Simon

Beverly Simon

Marketing/Senior Project Manager

GRANT OLIVER
7119 W. Morgan Ave.
Louisville, KY 41313
209-781-9301
oliverg@cityone.com

August 21, 20____

Margaret Harrison
SIMON AND JORDAN
381 Warner Drive, Suite 109
Louisville, KY 41319

Dear Ms. Harrison:

Your ad in today's <u>Louisville Journal</u> for a Senior Project Coordinator for direct mail and other marketing projects interests me for several reasons. I have the requisite skills and experience specified in your announcement. I know the direct mail market well and really enjoy this type of work. And I have over five years of experience in both direct mail and insurance marketing.

Since graduating with a BA in communication eight years ago, I have acquired progressively responsible experience in the direct mail and advertising fields. I have strong copywriting skills that are represented in the enclosed samples of my work. I also enjoy working with details. I am especially knowledgeable about demographics and list selection, and manage to juggle a variety of activities to meet deadlines.

Please consider the accompanying resume and work samples to be an application for this position. I will call you on Wednesday morning to answer any questions you may have about my candidacy.

Sincerely,

Grant Oliver

Grant Oliver

Meeting Planner

811 Weston Road
Detroit, MI 48123

June 5, 20____

Leslie Bailey
Catering Manager
V.I.P. CLUB
491 Main Street
Detroit, MI 48130

Dear Ms. Bailey:

I enclose my resume in response to your ad in the <u>Detroit Sun</u> for a Meeting Planner. As the largest private club in Detroit, the V.I.P. Club's reputation as one of the area's finest operations with large meeting facilities is well deserved. I know this is a very important position for your organization.

During the past three years I have worked as an Assistant Meeting Planner with the Detroit Convention Center. My work involved booking banquet groups, contacting clients, and marketing meeting services. I really enjoy this type of work, especially the details of getting groups scheduled and organized for events and solving problems of clients.

I would appreciate an opportunity to interview for this position. I plan to call your office on Friday morning to answer any questions you may have about my application for this position.

Sincerely,

Robert Gillian

Robert Gillian
gillianr@aol.com

Mortgage Banking/Loan Officer

4219 Gadwell Place
Virginia Beach, VA 23492

September 16, 20____

Jeffrey Allen
JEFFERSON MORTGAGE COMPANY
1873 Granby Street
Norfolk, VA 23500

Dear Mr. Allen:

As a Loan Officer at Commonwealth Bank, I originated more loans than any other employee in the past five years. That's why I think we should discuss the position you advertised in today's Virginia Pilot.

I enclose a resume which you requested. If you will give me a few minutes of your time, I believe it will be more than worth your while. I'll share with you one of my best kept secrets as to why I will most likely become a top performer at Jefferson Mortgage Company, too.

I'll call your office next Wednesday to see if you are interested in scheduling an interview to discuss my role at Jefferson Mortgage Company.

Sincerely,

Wanda Wright

Wanda Wright
wwright@bellatlantic.net

Nurse Practitioner

8115 West 11th St.
Evanston, IL 60012
August 11, 20____

Betty Clarke, RN
Nurse Recruiter
THE NEUROLOGY CENTER
27 Sheridan Road
Evanston, IL 60015

Dear Ms. Clarke:

The accompanying resume is in response to your ad in today's
Chicago Sun Times for a Nurse Practitioner. Given my past
training, experience, and professional interests, this is the type
of challenging position I most enjoy.

During the past five years I have worked as a Nurse Practitioner in
the neurological unit of Evanston General Hospital. I was responsible for direct patient care with an emphasis on patient teaching and
family/community education. I also helped develop the Bladder and
Bowel Management Program at Evanston General. I believe you are
planning to develop a similar program at your Center.

I am interested in continuing my career with a large private
neurological practice. Your organization has an outstanding reputation as a one of the country's foremost neurological programs. I
would like to contribute to the work of such a professional team.

I will call you on Thursday morning to answer any questions you
may have concerning my application.

Sincerely,

Valerie Young

Valerie Young
valeriey@aol.com

Occupational Therapist

717 Georgia Avenue
Indianapolis, IN 48712

March 1, 20____

Barry Bates
Human Resources
GREATER INDIANAPOLIS
    GENERAL HOSPITAL
67100 Conners Road
Indianapolis, IN 48712

Dear Mr. Bates:

Please consider my resume as an application for the Occupational
Therapist position you advertised in today's <u>Indianapolis Journal</u>.

As a recent graduate and licensed therapist, I believe I am well
qualified for this entry-level position. Prior to completing my degree
and becoming licensed, I worked as a paramedic and volunteer
health worker. Confronting numerous trauma cases involving auto
accidents, I decided I really wanted to work on rehab and acute care
cases in a hospital setting. Completing the degree and becoming a
licensed therapist is a dream come true.

I would appreciate an opportunity to interview for this position.
The acute care unit at Greater Indianapolis General Hospital has a
well deserved reputation for excellent patient care. I know, since I
visited there numerous times with patients. I would be proud to
join in contributing to the team effort.

I will call you on Friday morning to see if you have any questions
about my candidacy. I look forward to meeting with you and your
staff.

Sincerely,

Susan Wright

Susan Wright
<u>susanwright@planetone.com</u>

Office Manager/Bookkeeper

1801 Morton Lane
Detroit, MI 48723

September 23, 20____

FAXED TO: 319-393-2984

I read with interest your ad in today's <u>Detroit Sun</u> for an Office Manager/Bookkeeper. The accompanying resume summarizes my experience relevant to the qualifications you outlined.

Please note that I have served as both an office manager and bookkeeper for more than 12 years. Most of my experience is with the printing industry. I have supervised a staff of eight, performed general ledger functions, and am experienced in using Lotus 1-2-3. I love working with details, and I consistently meet my deadlines.

Since your ad did not include a company name nor address, I would appreciate it if you could give me more information about your organization and its location. The ad mentioned a printing company. I assume you are located in the Detroit area since we are in the same area code to which I am faxing this letter and resume.

I look forward to learning more about your company.

Sincerely,

Donald Reid

Donald Reid
Fax 319-281-3192
<u>reidd@aol.com</u>

Optometric Assistant

197 Memphis Road
Knoxville, TN 38239

September 12, 20____

Dr. Winston Solane
SOLANE OPTICAL CO.
712 W. Memphis Ave.
Knoxville, TN 38241

Dear Dr. Winston:

According to your ad in today's <u>Knoxville Times</u>, you are looking for someone to assist a Visual Therapist. As requested, I enclose a copy of my resume for your reference.

I have two years of optical experience as both a frame stylist and an assistant to a Visual Therapist. I am familiar with most aspects of an optical business and I work well with customers. I worked extremely well with the Visual Therapist when I was employed at Westview Optical Company. Please feel free to contact my previous employer (John Steffle, Tel. 389-2899), who found me to be exceptionally cooperative and who frequently received positive feedback from his customers about my work.

Your ad also requested salary requirements. I'm unable to give you a figure at this time. My salary requirements are flexible, depending on the nature of the work and responsibilities. I really need to know more about the position and your company before I can respond to salary issues and questions.

I look forward to learning more about this position and how my skills can best meet your needs.

Sincerely,

Jodie Murphy

Jodie Murphy
<u>murphyj@aol.com</u>

Paralegal

241 West Laramie
Albany, NY 14988

October 2, 20_____

Box M1230
ALBANY RECORD
Albany, NY 14992-1283

Your ad in today's newspaper caught my attention because it specified someone with FCC experience and a student who might be attending law school at night. As the accompanying resume indicates, my interests, experience, and schedule may be ideally suited to your needs.

My FCC experience was acquired during the past two years while working in Washington, DC on Capitol Hill as a Legislative Aide to Representative Wilson. I was responsible for developing legislative proposals relevant to FCC operations. In the process of doing this work I became very familiar with the day-to-day operations of the FCC. Many of my FCC contacts are still in place.

When Representative Wilson unexpectedly lost his bid for re-election, I immediately returned to Albany. I decided to study law at the University of Albany and enrolled as an evening student. My long-term plans are to pursue a law career in the Albany area.

I would appreciate an opportunity to interview for this position. I believe you will find my Capitol Hill and FCC experience to be a real plus in working with your firm.

Sincerely,

Harold Stevenson

Harold Stevenson
stevensonh@aol.com

Parks and Recreation Director

SYLVIA WHITEHURST   whitehursts@aol.com

8712 Graham Blvd.   Staunton, VA 23212   703-183-2314

January 14, 20____

Edward Jason
Personnel Administration
CITY OF CHARLESTON
P.O. Box 2918
Charleston, WV 25331

Dear Mr. Jason:

I read with interest your ad in the <u>Washington Post</u> for a Parks and Recreation Director. I am especially interested in this position because I have held a similar position here in Virginia. Having accomplished my goals in my present position, I'm now looking for another challenge in the parks and recreation field.

As indicated on the accompanying resume, I have a master's degree in Parks and Recreation, two years experience as Assistant City Manager, and four years experience as the Parks and Recreation Director in Staunton, Virginia. As Director, I

- directed all phases of community recreational programs and public grounds
- supervised a staff of 26
- prepared and administered a $1.2 million annual budget

I have very much enjoyed my work in Staunton. I have a solid record of accomplishment. Since I took over as the Parks and Recreation Director, public use of the community's recreational facilities has increased by 45%. We have been able to meet increased demands with only a 15% increase in the parks and recreation budget. We have done this through an innovative volunteer instructional program that has eliminated the need for additional staff to operate summer recreational programs.

I would appreciate an opportunity to interview for this position. I will call your office on Tuesday afternoon to see if your schedule would permit us to meet. Since I will be visiting Charleston during the week of January 24, perhaps we could meet at that time.

Sincerely,

Sylvia Whitehurst

Sylvia Whitehurst

Parts Manager

8149 Superior Avenue
Duluth, MN 50139

March 2, 20____

Lee Fuller
POWER RENTAL CO.
718 W. 24th St.
Duluth, MN 51039

Dear Mr. Fuller:

Please accept the enclosed resume as my application in response to your
ad in today's <u>Duluth Times</u> for a Parts Manager. You stated you
needed an experienced manager who has worked with large equipment
and who is familiar with ordering inventory and managing personnel.

I believe I have the necessary experience and skills to do this job well.
During the past 15 years I have worked at all levels and in a variety of
positions in the parts business. I began in receiving, moved on to
manage a stockroom, took customer orders, and managed a parts
warehouse with 13 employees. I'm experienced in operating
computerized inventory systems. In my current job I decreased
warehouse labor costs by 35% by installing a new inventory system.

I would appreciate the opportunity to interview for this position. Please
expect a phone call from me on Thursday afternoon. I'll be calling for
more information about the position as well as to answer any questions
you may have about my candidacy.

Sincerely,

Vick Russell

Vick Russell
<u>russellv@aol.com</u>

Pension Plan Administrator

ELIZABETH CARSON   carsone@earthweb.net

813 S. 9th Street   Columbus, MO 62351   819-231-3091

November 3, 20____

Bernard Graham
B. C. SYSTEMS, INC.
3819 Industrial Place
Columbus, MO 62350

Dear Mr. Graham:

I learned about your vacancy for a Pension Plan Administrator in this month's issue of <u>JobMarket</u>. As requested, I enclose a copy of my resume for your reference.

I have seven years of "hands on" experience as a Pension Plan Administrator. I am knowledgeable in pension law and regulations and experienced in handling defined contribution and defined benefit plans. My responsibilities have included checking, participant recordkeeping, 550 preparation, and client contact. I also have a CPA.

You may be interested in the new automated pension plan system I was instrumental in developing for my present employer. It reduced administrative costs by nearly 30% within the first two years of operation.

Please let me know if you need any additional information. I will call your office on Monday afternoon to see if you have questions about my candidacy.

Sincerely,

Elizabeth Carson

Elizabeth Carson

Property Manager

(special "T" letter format)

2932 Lottery Lane
St. Louis, MO 64321
June 3, 20____

Wendall Stone
R.L. PROPERTIES
671 Archway Blvd.
St. Louis, MO 64333

Dear Mr. Wendall:

I found with interest your ad for a Property Manager in today's St. Louis Dispatch. As an experienced Property Manager, I would bring to this job the following qualifications:

Your Requirements	My Qualifications
■ Enjoy working with people	■ Seven years of progressive experience in customer service.
	■ Regularly cited in annual performance appraisal for "excellent people skills."
	■ Serve as a volunteer to raise funds for the United Way.
■ Energetic personality	■ Recognized by current employer as a "go-getter" who maintains a high energy level, even in stressful situations.
	■ Enjoy new challenges and meeting new people.
■ Strong attention to detail	■ Five years experience as a quality control inspector. Improved inspections by 40% within first six months.
	■ Supervised housing inspection teams. Achieved a 97% rating for excellence.

The enclosed resume further summarizes my qualifications. I would appreciate an opportunity to speak with you about this position. I'll call your office next Wednesday afternoon to answer any question you may have about my candidacy.

Sincerely,

Sarinah Tamlinson

Sarinah Tamlinson
tamlinsons@aol.com

Rehab Nurse

WANDA PETERS, RN
213 Padra Fara, Apt. 137
Manila, The Philippines
Tel. 011-82-283-447
Fax 011-82-283-292
petersw@philword.com

June 23, 20____

Doris Silverman, MS, RN
Nurse Recruiter
OREGON GENERAL REHAB CENTER
8187 Elkins Drive
Portland, OR 98309

Dear Ms. Silverman:

Your ad in last week's <u>Portland Times</u> caught my mother's attention. She clipped the ad and faxed it to me in Manila.

After nearly 25 years of service with the U.S. Navy, I will be retiring this month. I will be returning to Portland within the next three weeks.

When I saw your ad, I was very pleased to learn it was for a rehab nursing position in Portland. The skills and experience you outline for this position are exactly the ones I possess. During the past eight years I worked as part of a rehab team at three Naval health facilities – Washington, DC, Hawaii, and Subic Bay. I've worked closely with medical professionals, patients, and their families.

Please look over the enclosed resume and let me know if you need any additional information. My international fax number is 011-82-283-292. After July 15, I can be contacted directly in Portland: 178 W. Terrace, Portland, OR 98311, Tel. 717-891-3291.

I look forward to meeting with you to discuss how my skills and experience can best meet the needs of Oregon General Rehab Center.

Sincerely,

Wanda Peters

Wanda Peters, RN

Research Assistant

2714 East-West Highway
Washington, DC 20132

April 3, 20____

Rebecca Thomas
METROPOLITAN WASHINGTON
    COUNCIL OF GOVERNMENTS
777 No. Capitol St., NE, #101
Washington, DC 20002

Dear Ms. Thomas:

I'm very interested in the vacancy you advertised in today's <u>Washington Post</u> for a Research Assistant to study the region's solid waste management practices. I understand this position is for a 15-month period.

As a graduate with a B.S. in environmental science, I have conducted research relating to waste removal and management in the Washington, DC area while employed as a summer intern with R.C. Research Associates. My work involved surveying waste removal and recycling collection contracts, estimating waste generation rates, using computerized databases, and writing major sections of the final research report. I believe my research experience directly relates to the study for which you are recruiting a Research Assistant.

Please consider this letter and accompanying resume to be my application for this position. I'll call you on Monday afternoon to answer any questions you might have concerning my candidacy. I would be delighted to send you a copy of the final research report I helped complete on regional solid waste management.

Sincerely,

Gerald Edison

Gerald Edison
edisong@aol.com

Travel Consultant

DARRELL BAIRD
234 Wayfare Road
Madison, WI 53123
317-382-9831
darrellbaird@earthone.com

4912 Planter Place
Madison, WI 53122

May 19, 20____

Marlene Powers
Personnel Department
XSELL WORLD TRAVEL
391 Capitol Street
Madison, WI 53122

Dear Ms. Powers:

I have five years of experience as a travel agent. During the past two years I worked mainly with corporate clients.

Your ad in today's <u>Madison Times</u> for a Travel Consultant appears to fit nicely with my interests, skills, and experience. As indicated in the accompanying resume, I am an Apollo/Focal Point agent with ADS computer experience. Since many of my clients travel abroad, I have extensive experience in international travel operations. My previous employers praised my excellent telephone manner and my ability to take charge in stressful situations.

I would appreciate the opportunity to interview for this position. I will call you Monday afternoon to answer any questions you may have about my interests and experience.

Sincerely,

Darrell Baird

Darrell Baird

Word Processor

134 Marlow Street
Cincinnati, OH 45310

February 8, 20____

Sarah Anderson
Personnel Department
BENTON INTERNATIONAL
5541 Phillips Circle
Cincinnati, OH 45307

Dear Ms. Anderson:

I type 120wpm, I'm accurate, I'm proficient in Word, and I work well under pressure and with minimum supervision. Your ad in today's Cincinnati Star for a Word Processor states these as the desirable skills and qualities you hope to hire.

I have seven years of experience as a word processor. My last two employers also were contractors who faced numerous proposal deadlines that required dependable word processing capabilities. I've never missed a deadline and I willingly work overtime to get the job done.

I would appreciate an opportunity to interview for this position as well as demonstrate my word processing skills. I will call you on Friday to see if you wish to schedule such a meeting.

Sincerely,

Belinda Bower

Belinda Bower
bowerb@aol.com

7

Cover Letters for
Different Situations

WHILE THE COVER LETTERS in Chapter 6 were written in response to vacancy announcements, the various letters presented in this chapter respond to several different situations that you will most likely find yourself in while conducting your job search. These letters fall into four major categories:

- referral cover letters
- telephone follow-up cover letters
- cold turkey cover letters
- broadcast cover letters

Each of these letters follows a different set of principles and probabilities for effectiveness.

Four Types of Letters

Referral cover letters are similar to several letters appearing in Chapter 5: they are written in response to a referral from a contact. These should be your most effective cover letters, because they are most likely written in the absence of competition, and because your "contact" has already screened you for the employer. Unlike referral letters – which are designed to get you information, advice, and referrals – these letters are aimed at getting a job interview.

Telephone follow-up cover letters are written in reference to job leads uncovered from telephone conversations. If you use the telephone to develop job leads, you will undoubtedly write several of these cover letters. In most cases the "leads" you uncover through telemarketing will ask you to send a copy of your resume for their reference. While many of these requests are real and sincere and may lead to job interviews, others are polite ways of saying *"We are not interested but go ahead and send me something in writing if you wish."* Consequently, the effectiveness of these letters largely depends on the availability of real job vacancies.

Cold turkey cover letters are written without reference to a specific vacancy or the aid of a contact or referral. These are basically more personalized versions of the broadcast letter – they are addressed to a specific name. Don't expect many results from such letters, even with the help of the telephone follow-up. Employers hire in reference to specific vacancies – not in reference to nicely crafted resumes and letters. If they lack a vacancy, they will have little or no interest in your letter and resume. These letters merely play the probability game – sent out to hundreds of employers in the hope of uncovering a few vacancies which will soon arise or which were missed when surveying sources of job listings. While most of these letters are a waste of time and effort, occasionally you may receive a positive response as "luck comes your way."

> *Employers hire in reference to specific vacancies – not in reference to nicely crafted resumes and letters.*

Broadcast cover letters represent the ultimate "fishing expedition" for employers who may have job vacancies. Unless you are exceptionally well qualified and your timing is right, few if any of these letters ever result in a positive response. Some professional resume broadcasters claim a two to five percent conversion rate – the percent of the broadcast letters they mail to their special mailing lists that turn into interviews. However, we have yet to see more than one percent of these letters going beyond the standard perfunctory reply:

> *"Thank you for your inquiry. While we do not have a vacancy available at present, we will keep your resume on file should our personnel needs change in the future."*

Since the key to effectiveness is a real job vacancy coinciding with your qualifications, it may not make much difference what you say in broadcast cover letters. The content of a broadcast cover letter may do little to enhance your resume or transform you into a serious applicant. Not surprisingly, sending a resume without a broadcast cover letter may be just as effective.

Our advice on broadcast cover letters and resumes is simple: **use a strong opener to grab the reader's attention**. Above all, you want the reader to remember you and your resume. This should be an exercise in good advertising copy, complete with an attention-grabbing headline – the opening sentence and paragraph. Give it your best shot, but keep your expectations **very** low. Don't expect your telephone to begin ringing or your mailbox to fill up with positive responses. In the end, you probably have better things to do with your job search time. Concentrate, instead, on writing approach, thank you, and cover letters that respond to **real** job vacancies.

Similar to our examples in Chapter 6, the cover letters in this chapter, whenever possible, should end with a follow-up statement indicating what action you will take next. Again, the rule for making these letters effective is follow up, follow up, follow up, follow up.

Referral Cover Letter

THOMAS EVANS   evanst@aol.com

1901 Davis Road   Little Rock, AR 79831   719-319-4601

May 3, 20____

William Billings
Director of Training
MANAGEMENT TRAINERS INC.
319 Garner Street, Suite 130
Little Rock, AR 79831

Dear Mr. Billings:

Tracy Stevens recommended that I send you a copy of my resume. She said she spoke with you last week. You indicated that you might be looking for someone with a background in management training to work with two of your new clients.

I have nearly seven years of experience as both a training instructor and writer of management training materials. I have also written management training proposals which received funding through federal agencies. My instructional work has been with both government and corporate audiences ranging from entry-level to senior level executives.

I am prepared to teach a variety of one- to five-day intensive courses on the following management subjects:

- Program Evaluation
- Supervision
- Supervising Former Colleagues
- Managing Organizational Change
- Problem Solving and Decision Making
- Benchmarking
- Time Management
- Managing Effective Meetings
- Conducting Management Control Reviews

I consistently receive "Excellent" to "Outstanding" evaluations from training participants. Since Tracy is familiar with my work, she can give you additional information on my background, experience, and skills.

I will call your office next Friday to answer any questions you may have about my work and to learn more about your future hiring needs.

Sincerely,

Thomas Evans

Thomas Evans

Referral Cover Letter

2984 Independent Road
Wichita, KS 58722
April 19, 20___

Martha Williamson
MCR VIDEO PRODUCTIONS
8193 Center Street
Wichita, KS 58721

Dear Ms. Williamson:

Michael Thiel recommended that I send you a copy of my resume for your reference. He said he thought you might have an impending vacancy for a Computer Graphic Artist with experience in industrial video production. I have such a background.

I also enclose samples of my work. My background includes strong technical drawing and design skills. I regularly work with an Aurora 240 and MacIntosh. My formal training included work in animation.

Please let me know if you wish to see some of my other work. Since I've worked with Michael on previous video projects, he knows my work well. I'm sure he could answer any questions you may have about my qualifications.

I will call you on Tuesday to answer any questions you may have about my work. Perhaps we could get together to discuss your future graphic art needs.

Sincerely,

Grace Olson

Grace Olson
olsong@erols.com

Referral Cover Letter

BETTY HAUSER   hauserb@aol.com
332 Westview Road   New Haven, CT 03813   291-382-2333

July 19, 20____

Michael Daniels, Editor
SCIENCE TODAY
1893 W. 27th St.
New York, NY 10013

Dear Mr. Daniels:

Gerald Reiter, your fraternity brother at UMC, recommended that I contact you about a possible position as a technical editor. He said you had mentioned the possibility of a vacancy arising in the very near future.

The enclosed resume summarizes my six years of experience as a technical writer. As the technical editor for a small scientific journal, I did all editing as well as some writing. Most recently I was in charge of supervising two assistant technical editors for a large scientific journal. I am especially good at translating scientific expressions into lay language.

I would appreciate being considered for the position of technical editor should it become vacant. I will call you next Thursday concerning my interest in the position.

Sincerely,

Betty Hauser

Betty Hauser

Telephone Follow-Up Cover Letter

4381 Springfield Road
Charleston, WV 25841
December 3, 20____

Daryl James
ABLE TECHNOLOGY
813 Rockledge Drive
Charleston, WV 25841

Dear Mr. James:

Thanks so much for the taking the time to speak with me concerning your hiring needs. As you requested, I enclose my resume for your reference.

While you may not have an immediate need for a Computer Programmer, I would appreciate being kept in mind should your hiring needs change. As I mentioned over the phone, I have PL/1 and COBOL skills. In addition, I have over five years of experience with PRIME, FoxPro, UNIX, and X-Windows.

I'll check with you in a few weeks to see if your personnel situation has changed. I appreciate your consideration and look forward to meeting you at some later date.

Sincerely,

Steven Manley

Steven Manley
manleys@aol.com

Telephone Follow-Up Cover Letter

MARCIA ARMSTRONG
227 South 7th Street
Joliet, IL 60993
319-713-0091
armstrongm@ace.net

September 5, 20____

Shari Elkhart, Manager
FIRST ILLINOIS BANK
813 Tilden Parkway
Joliet, IL 60999

Dear Ms. Elkhart:

It was such a pleasure speaking with you today about your need for a Customer Service Representative. You indicated an impending vacancy as well as the possibility of creating another such position. As you requested, I'm enclosing a copy of my resume for your reference.

During the past three years I worked as a Customer Service Representative at Joliet Savings and Loan. There I was responsible for answering customer inquiries, opening new accounts, promoting new banking services, and handling customer complaints. I especially enjoyed working with new customers in familiarizing them with the institution's services.

I would appreciate being considered for one of your Customer Service Representative positions. I will call your office on Friday morning to answer any questions you may have about my interests and background.

Sincerely,

Marcia Armstrong

Marcia Armstrong

Telephone Follow-Up Cover Letter

781 Lincoln Highway
Springfield, IL 62881

May 30, 20____

Peter Weston
ALLIED HEALTHCARE
913 West Finley Avenue
Springfield, IL 62876

Dear Mr. Weston:

I very much enjoyed talking with you today about your need for a Senior EDP Auditor. Our conversation got me thinking about both your needs and my future.

I had no idea John Clarkson had suggested me as a possible candidate for this position. While I remember speaking with John recently about my interest in working with a healthcare organization, I have not been actively pursuing a job change nor seriously contemplating a major move within the near future. However, your phone call got me thinking again about making such a career move.

I enclose a copy of my resume which you requested. I have over 10 years of increasingly responsible accounting experience. During the past five years I have been in charge of the EDP Audit function at Keegan Systems, Inc. I developed and expanded the company's programs, conducted audits of its management information system, and expanded computerized audits. I have experience in auditing large IBM system computers.

Your phone call was the catalyst for rethinking my future here at Keegan Systems, Inc. I would appreciate meeting with you soon to discuss how my interests and experience might best benefit Allied Healthcare. I'll call you this time – Wednesday afternoon – to see if you are still interested in pursuing my candidacy. In the meantime, I will have a chance to do some more thinking about what I would like to achieve at Allied Healthcare.

I look forward to meeting you soon.

Sincerely,

Patricia Dooley

Patricia Dooley
dooleyp@ace.net

Cold Turkey Cover Letter

SHELTON HULL   hull@erols.com

159 Grand Avenue   Lincoln, NE 58271   713-820-6615

January 17, 20____

Julia Warner, Principal
LINCOLN HIGH SCHOOL
829 Main Street
Lincoln, NE 58270

Dear Ms. Warner:

Do you plan to hire Social Science teachers this coming year? If you do, I would appreciate being considered for a vacancy.

As indicated in the accompanying resume, I have a master's degree in Political Science and five years of high school teaching experience. While my teaching experience has been with Department of Defense schools in Europe, I do have a Nebraska teaching certificate which I acquired upon graduating from the University of Nebraska. I did my student teaching in Omaha, Nebraska.

After living abroad for five years, my wife and I now plan to settle in the Lincoln area to pursue high school teaching careers. I believe my overseas teaching experience would be a real asset to Lincoln High School's social science program, especially given the momentous changes taking place today in Europe.

I will call you within the next 10 days to see if your hiring needs coincide with my training and experience. I appreciate your consideration.

Sincerely,

Shelton Hull

Shelton Hull

Cold Turkey Cover Letter

198 Cherokee Trail
Marietta, GA 30932

October 3, 20____

Louis Paris
PARIS ADVERTISING
3901 Pickney Street
Marietta, GA 30930

Dear Mr. Paris:

Congratulations on receiving this year's Jaycee Award for outstanding businessperson in Marietta. Succeeding in the advertising business indeed deserves recognition and applause. It's a tough business requiring tough and risky decisions. Above all, it requires talented people who know what they are doing. I know. I've been in the business for nearly 15 years.

When I read about your award in the Marietta Times, the article mentioned you were in the process of expanding your 22-employee firm to 30 employees. Would I be correct in assuming you will be looking for new talent?

I enclose a copy of my resume for your reference. I know the advertising business inside out. I've worked with both small and large firms and managed both small business and corporate accounts.

Could we meet at some mutually convenient time to discuss our mutual interests? I'll call your office next Thursday to see if your schedule would permit such a meeting.

Sincerely,

Charlene Parker

Charlene Parker
parkerc@aol.com

Cold Turkey Cover Letter

PORTER MACKEL
3891 Terrace Lawn
Jacksonville, FL 35817
319-721-3827
mackelp@net2.com

October 3, 20____

Martin Shephard
SOUTHERN REALTY
8189 King Street
Jacksonville, FL 35819

Dear Mr. Shephard:

Whoever said you can't get rich quick never met someone who made their fortune in real estate. While I may not be rich now, I hope to be soon. And it will be made in real estate working with one of the top agencies.

I've been a real estate agent for nearly four years. Last year I joined the $2 million club. Next year I plan to be in the $5 million club.

If you are looking for a top performer who knows how to sell and sell and sell, then we should talk soon. In the meantime, I enclose a copy of my resume for your reference.

I will call your office on Thursday afternoon to see if your schedule would permit us to meet in the very near future. Since I'm planning to move to another real estate firm within the next two months, I would really like to learn more about your firm and how I might fit into your plans for the future.

Sincerely,

Porter Mackel

Porter Mackel

Broadcast Cover Letter

GENE STALLINGS

---

291 Tremont Road   312-713-3921
Chicago, IL 60015   stallingsg@ace.com

October 6, 20____

Sales professional gets immediate results . . . you can bank on!

Would you like to see your sales increase by 30% within three months? You need not look further. I increased sales by 30% within three months of taking over and reorganizing our district sales force. I believe I can do the same for you.

The accompanying resume summarizes what I have done for others. If you are interested in what I can do for you, please call me at 312-713-3921.

Sincerely,

Gene Stallings

Gene Stallings

Broadcast Cover Letter

<u>DAVID MARTIN</u>   713 Montgomery Ave.   St. Paul, MN 58219
                           717-389-9182   martin@erols.com

July 30, 20____

When was the last time you heard an employee say this? *"I'm not performing up to my ability, but I promise you will see some major changes within the next three weeks."* I said this last year to my employer.

Three years ago I was so unhappy with my job that I nearly quit. I just didn't have the same level of enthusiasm and drive that I had in previous years. I thought maybe I should start a new career or just take off for a year to figure out what I really wanted to do with the rest of my life. Instead, I decided to rethink how I was doing my present job and perhaps reinvent my chosen career. Expecting to be fired, I went to my boss and told her I was unhappy with my performance. She was surprised at hearing such a confession since she considered me to be above average in comparison to other employees. I told her I could do much better than "above average," and I asked if I could take two weeks off to rethink what I really wanted to do. She agreed and I did my thinking.

It was the best two weeks I ever spent. I decided it was time to do things differently. I sat down and specified two goals I wanted to achieve over the next few years and five related goals to target over the new three months. Then I detailed how I would implement each goal and visualized the final outcomes in terms of percentage increases in productivity.

I returned to work with renewed enthusiasm and drive. Within two months I achieved my three-month goals. I repeated this goal setting and visualizing exercise again and again until it is now automatically embedded into my daily routines.

I am no longer an "above average" employee. I am the top performer. My productivity has increased by more than 50%. I enjoy my work more than ever and look forward to each day with renewed energy.

If you are planning to expand your team to include more self-directed employees, please give me a call. I have more than 10 years of increasingly responsible experience in marketing. I believe I can do for you what I have done for previous employers – take charge and improve profitability. I'll tell you the truth about what I am doing, where I am going, and what I need to do to make my work better than ever.

Let's talk the next time you have a vacancy for someone with my goals and experience.

Sincerely,

David Martin

David Martin

Broadcast Cover Letter

JANICE WHITE   janicewhite@ace.com

8314 River Run   Pittsburgh, PA 17382   415-892-9831

June 7, 20____

What a great place to work!

That's what I and many others said only seven months ago – and then the sky fell. Who would have guessed that within three months Jamison Department Store would file Chapter 11 and then close its doors in another three months. A leveraged buyout engineered in New York City unfortunately killed what was one of Pittsburgh's finest department stores. Many former employees are still in shock.

I had six great years at Jamison's. I was responsible for the home furnishings department. We put on some wonderful special displays that nearly doubled our floor traffic during my last two years at Jamison's. In fact, my department was the second highest profit center for the Pittsburgh branch of Jamison's.

I am writing to you in the hope that you might have a current or forthcoming vacancy for someone with my interests, skills, and experience. If so, give me a call. I'm willing to relocate for the right challenge.

Sincerely,

Janice White

Janice White

8

Resume Letters As Job Applications

RESUME LETTERS ARE BOTH a particular type of letter and a special type of resume. Focusing on the requirements of a particular position, these letters are usually written in lieu of the traditional cover letter/resume combination. As such, a resume letter incorporates the experience sections of your resume in the format of an approach or application letter.

A Kind of Customized Resume

Resume letters have one major advantage over the more traditional letter-resume combination: they enable the writer to customize a resume and letter in reference to the specific needs of employers. They are similar in many respects to one of our most powerful job search letters – "T" letters (see examples on pages 133 and 148). Resume letters are especially important if the objective on your resume does not seem to fit the needs of the employer. A resume letter, which includes a more precise employer-sensitive objective, may serve you better than your generic resume.

Resume letters also have one major disadvantage: they don't look like resumes and thus may weaken your application. Individuals expecting to receive a cover letter and resume combination may view your resume letter as incomplete because it does not contain all the information they expect to receive in the traditional cover letter/resume combination.

Resume letters can be written for all types of job search situations. They can respond to vacancy announcements or function as cold turkey and broadcast letters, or as referral and telephone follow-up letters.

The examples in this chapter respond to different situations. Be sure to include a follow-up statement in your resume letter. Your phone call can make the difference between your resume just getting a perfunctory reading versus being responded to in the form of a job interview and perhaps a job offer.

Cold Turkey
(Research/Writing/Publications)

773 Main Street
Williamsburg, VA 23572

November 12, 20____

Barbara Thompson, President
SRM ASSOCIATES
421 91st Street
New York, NY 11910

Dear Ms. Thompson:

I just completed reading the article in <u>Business Today</u> on SRM Associates. Your innovative approach to recruiting minorities is of particular interest to me because of my background in public relations and minority recruitment.

I am interested in learning more about your work as well as the possibility of joining your firm. My qualifications include:

- research and writing on minority recruitment and medical education
- secured funding and administered $845,000 minority representation program
- published several professional articles and reports on creative writing, education, and minorities
- organized and led public relations, press, and minority conferences
- M.A. in Journalism and B.A. in English

I will be in New York City during the week of December 10. Perhaps your schedule would permit us to meet briefly to discuss our mutual interests. I will call your office next week to see if such a meeting can be arranged.

I appreciate your consideration.

Sincerely yours,

Michele R. Folger

Michele R. Folger
<u>folgerm@ace.com</u>

Cold Turkey
(Trainer/Computers)

4921 Tyler Drive
Washington, DC 20011

March 15, 20_____

Doris Stevens
STR CORPORATION
179 South Trail
Rockville, MD 21101

Dear Ms. Stevens:

STR Corporation is one of the most dynamic computer companies in the nation. Its model employee training and development program makes it the type of organization I am interested in joining.

I am seeking a training position with a computer firm which would use my administrative, communication, and planning abilities to develop effective training and counseling programs. My experience includes:

- Administration: Supervised instructors and counselors. Coordinated job vacancy and training information for businesses and schools.

- Communication: Conducted over 100 workshops on interpersonal skills, stress management, and career planning. Frequent guest speaker to various agencies and private firms. Experienced writer of training manuals and public relations materials.

- Planning: Planned and developed counseling programs for over 5,000 employees. Reorganized interviewing and screening processes and developed program of individualized and group counseling.

I am also completing my Ph.D. in industrial psychology with an emphasis on developing training and counseling programs for technical personnel.

Could we meet to discuss your program as well as how my experience might relate to your needs? I will call your office on Tuesday morning, March 23, to arrange a convenient time.

I especially want to show you a model employee counseling and career development program I recently developed. Perhaps you may find it useful for your work with STR.

Sincerely,

James C. Astor

James C. Astor
astorj@earthweb.com

Vacancy Announcement
(Sales/Information Processing)

136 West Davis St.
Sacramento, CA 98771
September 5, 20____

Vicki Beatress
S.R. SYSTEMS
893 Mountain View Road
Sacramento, CA 98777

Dear Ms. Beatress:

I read with interest your ad in today's <u>Sacramento Star</u> for a Sales Associate. I'm especially interested in this position because of my previous experience in working with copy machines and corporate clients. I have been both a user and promoter of your systems.

My experience and qualifications include seven years of progressive experience in the following positions:

- <u>Sales associate</u>: Represented both Toshiba and Ricoh copy machines to corporate clients. Increased corporate accounts by 30% within 18 months. Recognized as the top Toshiba salesperson for the past three years. Linotech Systems, 2002 to present.

- <u>Office Manager</u>: Performed office management responsibilities. Planned and re-organized service center. Initiated time and cost studies which saved company $40,000 in additional labor costs. MCT Corporation (Vancouver, WA), 1997 to 2001.

I also recently completed my bachelor's degree in business and computer science.

I believe my interests, skills, and experience are a good fit for this position. May I call you on Wednesday afternoon to answer any questions you may have concerning my candidacy?

Sincerely,

Wayne Watson

Wayne Watson
<u>watsonw@aol.com</u>

Vacancy Announcement
(Architectural Drafter)

1099 Seventh Avenue
Akron, OH 44522
February 1, 20____

Michael Abrams
THE LIGHTNER COMPANY
8113 Grand Avenue
Akron, OH 44520

Dear Mr. Abrams:

I am very interested in the Architectural Drafter position you advertised in today's <u>Akron Beacon Journal</u>. This is exactly the type of position I have been seeking. It fits nicely with my technical knowledge and practical experience for enhancing construction design and building operations.

I would bring to this position nearly 10 years of progressively responsible experience in all phases of construction design:

- <u>Draftsman</u>: Akron Construction Company, Akron. Helped develop construction plans for $14 million of residential and commercial construction. (2002 to present)

- <u>Drafting Assistant/Apprentice</u>: R.T. Design Company, Akron. Served as an apprentice in helping design residential developments. Worked on the $130-million Lakeview Estate Development Center. (1998 to 2001)

- <u>Cabinetmaker</u>: Jason's Linoleum and Carpet Company, Akron. Designed and constructed kitchen countertops and cabinets; installed the material in homes; cut and laid linoleum flooring in apartment complexes. (1996 to 1997)

- <u>Carpenter's Assistant</u>: Kennison Associates, Akron. Assisted carpenter in the reconstruction of a restaurant and in building of forms for pouring concrete. (Summer 1995)

My training background includes completion of 15 hours of drafting courses at the Akron Vocational and Training Center.

I appreciate your consideration. I will call you on Monday afternoon to answer any questions you may have about my candidacy.

Sincerely,

John Albert

John Albert
albertj@aol.com

Referral
(Public Relations/Conference Coordinator)

1234 Main Street
Norfolk, VA 23508

April 30, 20____

Dale Roberts
Business Manager
VIRGINIA BEACH CONVENTION CENTER
2981 Ocean Boulevard
Virginia Beach, VA 23519

Dear Mr. Roberts:

A mutual acquaintance of ours, Paul Amos, suggested that I contact you about the new Virginia Beach Convention Center. He remarked that you are developing a comprehensive public relations and marketing plan to attract convention business.

As an officer of my local chapter and regional division of Toastmasters International, I have acquired a substantial amount of public relations, special events planning, and program coordination experience. Along with my professional work, my background includes working with diverse audiences, developing publicity campaigns and promotional materials, marketing services and benefits, recruiting new members, handling financial records, and meeting important deadlines. Furthermore, I have experience in writing and giving speeches, chairing work groups, representing organizations, creative writing, and teaching.

Since I have a strong interest in public relations-type activities and have a thorough knowledge of our region and its resources, I was quite interested to hear that your new marketing plan may use conference coordinators to work with your sales staff. I would be very interested in learning more about your plans and exploring future possibilities.

I plan to be near your office next week and wonder if we could have a brief meeting? I'll give your office a call in the next few days to see if a mutually convenient time could be arranged.

Sincerely,

Karen Jones

Karen Jones
karenjones@ace.com

Vacancy Announcement
(Management Information Systems)

2238 South Olby Road
Sacramento, CA 97342
May 22, 20____

Dorothy Avery
C.R. MANAGEMENT SYSTEMS
3817 Jefferson Street
Peoria, IL 61433

Dear Ms. Avery:

Your ad in today's <u>Peoria Journal Star</u> for a Management Information System Specialist caught my interest because it is ideally suited to my background.

I believe my past 15 years of work with the U.S. Navy in Systems Analysis and Management Information Systems has prepared me well for this position:

- <u>Engineering Technician</u>: Reviewed technical publications to improve operational and technical descriptions and maintenance procedures. Developed system operation training course for high-level, nontechnical managers. Developed PERT charts for scheduling 18-month overhauls. Implemented a planning maintenance program and schedule for computer complex to reduce equipment down-time and increase utilization by user departments. (2002 to present)

- <u>Assistant Manager/System Technicians</u>: Established and coordinated preventive/corrective maintenance system for four missile guidance systems resulting in increased reliability. Advised management on system operation and utilization for maximum effectiveness. Performed system test analysis and directed corrective maintenance actions. Interfaced with other managers to coordinate interaction of equipment and personnel. Conducted maintenance and safety inspections of various types of work centers. (1999 to 2001).

- <u>Assistant Manager/System Technician</u>: Supervised system tests, analyzed results, and directed maintenance actions on two missile guidance systems. Overhauled and adjusted within factory specifications two special purpose computers, reducing down-time over 50%. Established and coordinated system and computer training program. Received the "Battle Efficiency E For Excellence" award in competition with other units. (1996 to 1998).

I would appreciate an opportunity to speak with you about how my experience can best meet your needs. I will call you on Wednesday to answer any questions.

Sincerely,

Gary Platt

Gary Platt
<u>plattg@earthone.net</u>

Referral
(Criminal Justice)

CHERYL AYERS   ayersc@aol.com

2589 Jason Drive   Ithaca, NY 14850   208-467-8735

April 20, 20____

Robert Byers
LAW ENFORCEMENT INSTITUTE
9881 Erie Road, Suite 203
Buffalo, NY 15283

Dear Mr. Byers:

Maryann Wilkerson, who interned with your department last year, suggested that I write to you concerning my interest in a research, data analysis, and planning position in law enforcement administration. She said you were planning to convert one of your internship positions to an entry-level position for a recent college graduate.

I will be graduating from Ithaca College in June with a B.S. in Criminal Justice. I majored in Law Enforcement Administration and minored in Management Information Systems. My G.P.A. is 3.6/4.0.

While my professional work experience is limited, I would bring to your organization the following demonstrated skills:

- <u>Leadership</u>: Head secretary while working at State Police (past two years). Served as Rush Chair and Social Chair for Chi Phi Sorority. Elected Captain and Co-Captain three times during 10 years of cheerleading.

- <u>Responsibility</u>: Handled highly confidential information, material, and files for State Police. Aided in the implementation of on-line banking system. In charge of receiving and dispersing cash funds for drive-in restaurant.

- <u>Organization</u>: Revised ticket system for investigators' reports at State Police. Planned schedules and budget, developed party themes and skits, obtained prop material, and coordinated work of others during sorority rush.

- <u>Data Analysis</u>: Program in Fortran and Cobal. Analyzed State Police data on apprehensions and wrote final report.

I would appreciate an opportunity to interview for this position. I will call you on Wednesday afternoon to answer any questions you may have about my candidacy.

Sincerely,

Cheryl Ayers

Cheryl Ayers

Telephone Follow Up

(Research)

MICHELE R. FOLGER
733 Main Street
Williamsburg, VA 23572
803-376-9932
folgerm@ace.com

September 27, 20____

Eric Johnson
THE POLICY INSTITUTE
1873 M Street, NW
Washington, DC 20037

Dear Mr. Johnson:

Thanks so much for taking the time to talk with me today about my interest in a research position with your organization. I learned a great deal about the Institute's work.

As I mentioned over the phone, I have over six years of research and program development experience with urban policy issues. This includes:

- Program Development: Conducted research on the representation of minority students in medical colleges. Developed proposal for a major field study. Secured funding for a $845,000 project. Coordinated and administered the program which had major effect on medical education in the New York project area. Initiated and developed a national minority student recruitment program for 20 medical colleges.

- Writing: Compiled and published reports in a variety of education areas. Produced several booklets on urban problems for general distribution. Published more than 20 articles in professional journals. Wrote and presented numerous conference papers.

- Research: Gathered and analyzed information concerning higher education in a variety of specialized fields. Familiar with computers and the latest data collection and statistical methods.

I enclose a sample of my work ("Representation of Minority Medical Students") for your reference. The article appears in the October issue of Medical Educator.

I will call you next week to answer any questions you may have about my interests, skills, and experience.

Sincerely,

Michele R. Folger

Michele R. Folger

Broadcast
(Publishing/Computers)

MARY FURNISS
7812 W. 24th St.   821-879-1124
Dallas, TX 71234   furnissm@aol.com

September 11, 20____

Do you ever wonder why some publishers accomplish the same production tasks for $500,000 less than others?

Three years ago I found an answer to this question which has now saved my employer more than $1 million. I may be able to do the same for you in this and other computer-related areas.

With over 10 years of experience in the publishing industry, I am now looking for a challenging opportunity that would build upon my previous experience:

- Computer Applications Manager: Managed all computer-related projects for publishing firm with annual sales of $40 million. Presented yearly capital expenditure and general systems budget, negotiated computer service contracts, evaluated and recommended new equipment and software purchases, and trained staff to use software and hardware. Replaced ATEX typesetting with desktop publishing system that immediately saved the company $650,000 in operational costs. Stevens Publishing Company, Fort Worth, TX, 2001 to present.

- Editorial/Production Supervisor: Supervised all computer-related projects. Trained staff of 27 to use WordPerfect and other software applications. Devised an innovative system that transformed traditional galley editing into an efficient electronic editing system. New computerized system eliminated the need for two additional employees to handle the traditional galley editing system. Reduced errors by 70 percent. Benton Publishing Company, San Francisco, CA, 1998-2000

- Editorial Assistant: Prepared annual Encyclopedia of International Forestry materials for editing and production. Supervised freelancers for special editorial projects. Proofread and copy-edited materials for 18 books produced annually. Received "Employee of the Year" award for initiating a new computerized editing system that saved the company $70,000 in annual freelance editing fees. Benton Publishing Company, San Francisco, CA, 1996-1997

If my skills fit your needs, I would love to talk to you about the possibility of joining your team on either a part-time or full-time basis. Please give me a call.

Sincerely,

Mary Furniss

Mary Furniss

Vacancy Announcement
(Construction/Project Manager)

7781 West Gate Road
Cincinnati, OH 44411
March 22, 20____

Martin Drew
CONNERS CONSTRUCTION CO.
6661 Rowling Rock Rd.
Cincinnati, OH 44410

Dear Mr. Drew:

My skills and experience perfectly coincide with your announcement in today's <u>Cincinnati Observer</u> for a Project Manager. I am seeking a challenging project management position that would use my demonstrated skills to complete projects in a timely and cost-effective manner.

I would bring to this position 28 years of progressively responsible construction management experience involving all facets of construction, from start-up to final inspection. I am experienced in supervising all aspects of construction including masonry, concrete work, carpentry, electrical, mechanical, and plumbing. In addition, I communicate and work well with individuals at all levels, from clients to a diverse mix of architects and subcontractors.

Highlights of my career include:

- <u>Independent Contractor, Barstow & Thomas</u>: Owned and managed a general contracting company doing $8 million in commercial construction each year. Performed all estimating, established contacts with subcontractors, purchased specialty items and materials, and handled shop drawings. Completed most jobs within 30 days of projected completion dates and managed to keep costs 5 percent under estimates. Cincinnati, 1988 to 2004.

- <u>Job Superintendent, J.P. Snow</u>: Supervised all work from start-up to final inspection as well as established all time schedules from start to finish. Handled shop drawings, lab testing, job testing, change orders, daily reports, job progress reports, payroll, and hiring. Initiated an innovative scheduling system that saved the employer more than $60,000 in projected down-time. Consistently praised for taking initiative, providing exceptional leadership, and communicating well with clients, architects, and subcontractors. Columbus, 1977 to 1987.

I would appreciate an opportunity to interview for this position. I will call you Tuesday afternoon to answer any questions you may have about my candidacy.

Sincerely,

James Barstow

James Barstow
<u>barstowj@earthone.com</u>

Referral

(Accountant)

443 West Capitol Street
Houston, TX 78261
March 4, 20____

Judith Holderman
SIMON AND TUCKER
8813 Tower Avenue, Suite 413
Houston, TX 78269

Dear Ms. Holderman:

While visiting my neighbor yesterday, I met Wendy Watson. After learning I was in the process of making a job change, she suggested I contact you. She mentioned you were recruiting for an Accounting/Finance position.

I have more than 10 years of increasingly responsible accounting/finance experience:

- Accountant: Analyzed accounting systems and installed new IBM ledger system for over 30 corporate accounts. Conducted training programs attended by more than 500 accountants with small businesses. Developed proposals, presented demonstration programs, and prepared reports for corporate clients. Increased new accounts by 42% over a four-year period. J.S. Conners & Co., Chicago, 2002 to present.

- Junior Accountant: Acquired extensive experience in all aspects of corporate accounting while assigned to the Controller's Office. Prepared detailed financial records for corporate meetings as well as performed basic accounting tasks such as journal entries, reconciling discrepancies, and checking records for accuracy and consistency. Assisted office in converting to a new computerized accounting system that eliminated the need for additional personnel and significantly improved the accuracy and responsiveness. Simon Electrical Co., Chicago, 1996 to 2000.

- Accounting Clerk: Acquired working knowledge of basic accounting functions for a 200+ employee organization with annual revenues of $45 million. Prepared journal vouchers, posted entries, and completed standard reports. Proposed a backup accounting system that was implemented by the Senior Accountant. Johnson Supplies, Chicago, 1993 to 1995.

Please let me know if you need any additional information. I will call you on Thursday afternoon to answer any questions you may have about my interests, skills, and experience.

Sincerely,

Mary Southern

Mary Southern
southernm@aol.com

Telephone Follow Up

(Paralegal)

771 Anderson Street
Knoxville, TN 38921

September 1, 20____

Mary Leonard
FORNAW, PETERS, AND LEWIS
3991 Jackson Blvd.
Knoxville, TN 38919

Dear Ms. Leonard:

Thank you for speaking with me today about opportunities in your firm for paralegals. Should a vacancy arise, I would appreciate being considered for a position in your firm. I would bring to your firm the following qualifications:

- <u>Law</u>: Completed 36 semester hours of criminal justice course work with special emphasis on criminal law. Served as an intern with law firm specializing in criminal law. Interviewed clients, drafted documents, conducted legal research, assisted lawyers in preparing court briefs. Participated in criminal justice forums sponsored by the Department of Criminal Justice at the University of Illinois.

- <u>Research</u>: Conducted research on several criminal cases as both a student and a paralegal intern. Experienced in examining court cases, interviewing lawyers and judges, and observing court proceedings. Proficient in using microfiche and computerized databases for conducting legal research.

- <u>Communication</u>: Prepared research papers, legal summaries, and memos, and briefed attorneys on criminal cases relevant to assignments. Used telephone extensively for interviewing clients and conducting legal research.

Please let me know if you need any additional information. I will periodically check with you concerning impending vacancies.

Sincerely,

Charles Davis

Charles Davis
<u>davisc@earthone.com</u>

Vacancy Announcement
(Bookkeeper)

997 Mountain Road
Denver, CO 80222
June 4, 20____

James Fountain
SIMON WALTERS, INC.
771 George Washington Blvd.
Denver, CO 80220

Dear Mr. Fountain:

I read with interest your ad in today's <u>Rocky Mountain Times</u> for a bookkeeper. I believe my experience may be ideally suited for this position:

- <u>Manager, Accounts Payable, T.L. Dutton, Denver</u>: Supervised 18 employees who routinely processed 200 invoices a day. Handled vendor inquiries and adjustments. Conducted quarterly accruals and reconciliations. Screened candidates and conducted annual performance evaluations. Reduced the number of billing errors by 30 percent and vendor inquiries by 25% within the first year. 2001 to present.

- <u>Supervisor, Accounts Payable, AAA Pest Control, Denver</u>: Supervised 10 employees who processed nearly 140 invoices a day. Audited vendor invoices, authorized payments, and balanced daily disbursements. Introduced automated accounts receivable system for improving the efficiency and accuracy of receivables. 1998 to 2000.

- <u>Bookkeeper, Davis Nursery, Ft. Collins</u>: Processed accounts payable and receivable, reconciled accounts, balanced daily disbursements, and managed payroll for a 20-employee organization with annual revenues of $1.8 million. 1995 to 1997.

- <u>Bookkeeper, Jamison's Lumber, Ft. Collins</u>: Assisted accountant in processing accounts payable and receivable and managing payroll for a 40-employee organization with annual revenues of $3.2 million. 1991-1994.

I am currently taking advanced courses in accounting, computer science, and management at Colorado Junior College in Denver.

I will call you on Thursday afternoon to answer any questions you may have concerning my candidacy.

Sincerely,

Jane Barrows

Jane Barrows
<u>barrowsj@erols.com</u>

Cold Turkey
(Computer Sales)

136 W. Davis St.
Washington, DC 20030

January 7, 20____

James C. Thomas, President
ADVANCED TECHNOLOGY CORP.
721 West Stevens Road
Bethesda, MD 20110

Dear Mr. Thomas:

Advanced Technology's computer systems are the finest on the market today. I know because I have used different systems over the past eight years. Your company is the type of organization I would like to be associated with.

Over the next few months I will be seeking a sales position with an information processing company. My technical, sales, and administrative experience include:

- Technical: Eight years operating a variety of computer systems for government and corporate clients.

- Sales: Recruited clients; maintained inventory; received and filled orders; improved business-community relations.

- Administrative: Planned and re-organized word processing center; created new tracking and filing systems; initiated time and cost studies which reduced labor costs by $30,000 and improved efficiency of operations.

In addition, I have a bachelor's degree in communication with an emphasis on public speaking, interpersonal communication, and psychology.

Your company interests me very much. I would appreciate an opportunity to meet with you to discuss how my qualifications can best meet your needs. I will call your office next Monday, January 18, to arrange a meeting with you at a convenient time.

Sincerely yours,

Gail S. Topper

Gail S. Topper
topperg@aol.com

Broadcast
(Financial Analyst)

SUSAN ALLEN   allens@ace.com
325 West End Street   Atlanta, GA 30019   402-378-9771

January 2, 20____

Are you looking for an investment analyst who will increase client investments by 20% each year? If so, let's talk about how I can do for you what I have done for previous employers.

With more than 10 years experience, I have a solid track record of performance. I would bring to your firm the following experience:

■ <u>Investment Analyst, First City Bank, Atlanta</u>: Managed $650 million in diverse portfolios for bank's major clients which averaged 12 percent annual return on investment. Regularly met with clients, reviewed current investments, and presented new investment options for further diversifying portfolios. Introduced biweekly newsletter for communicating investment strategies with clients and bank officers. 2000 to 2005.

■ <u>Research Analyst, Georgia Bank, Atlanta</u>: Conducted research, wrote reports, and briefed supervisor on stock market trends and individual companies which affected the bank's $1.2 billion securities portfolio. Worked closely with Investment Analyst in developing new approaches to communicating research findings and summary reports to clients and bank officers. 1997 to 1999.

■ <u>Research Assistant/Intern, Columbia Savings Bank, Columbia, SC</u>: Served as a Summer Intern while completing undergraduate degree. Assigned as Research Assistant to Chief Analyst. Followed stock market trends and conducted research on selected investment banks. 1996.

I also have an MBA from the University of Miami. Concentrating on finance and management, my thesis was entitled <u>Successful Investment Strategies of Florida's Ten Major Banks</u>.

Please give me a call if your hiring needs coincide with my interests, skills, and experience.

Sincerely,

Susan Allen

Susan Allen

Vacancy Announcement
(Sales Manager)

7723 Stevens Avenue
Phoenix, AZ 80023
August 23, 20____

Cindy Morrow
HINES DEPARTMENT STORE
1831 Desert Blvd.
Phoenix, AZ 80021

Dear Ms. Morrow:

I am responding to your ad in today's <u>Phoenix Sun</u> for a Sales Manager. I would bring to this position twelve years of progressively responsible experience in all phases of retail sales and marketing with major discount stores. I annually improved profitability by 15 percent and consistently rated in the top 10 percent of the workforce. My experience includes:

- <u>Sales Manager, K-Mart, Memphis, TN</u>: Managed four departments with annual sales of nearly $8 million. Hired, trained, and supervised a culturally diverse workforce of 14 full-time and 6 part-time employees. Reorganized displays, developed new marketing approaches, coordinated customer feedback with buyers in upgrading quality of merchandise, and improved customer service that resulted in 25 percent increase in annual sales. Received "Outstanding" performance evaluation and "Employee of the Year" award. 2002 to present.

- <u>Assistant Buyer, Wal-Mart, Memphis, TN</u>: Maintained inventory levels for three departments with annual sales of $5 million. Developed more competitive system of vendor relations that reduced product costs by 5 percent. Incorporated latest product and merchandising trends into purchasing decisions. Worked closely with department managers in maintaining adequate inventory levels for best-selling items. 1998 to 2001.

- <u>Salesperson, Zayres, Knoxville, TN</u>: Responsible for improving sales in four departments with annual sales of $3.5 million. Reorganized displays and instituted new "Ask An Expert" system for improved customer relations. Sales initiatives resulted in a 20 percent increase in annual sales. Cited for "excellent customer relations" in annual performance evaluation. Worked part-time while completing education. 1995 to 1997.

Please consider this letter to be my application for this position. I will call you next Friday morning to answer any questions you may have about my candidacy.

Sincerely,

Mark Able

Mark Able
<u>ablem@tocan.com</u>

Referral

(Military/Attorney)

STEVEN MARSH   *marshs@aol.com*

2001 West James Ct.   ▪   Seattle, WA 98322   ▪   501-789-4321

October 31, 20____

Morton Gates
BOEING CO.
1141 Washington Avenue
Seattle, WA 98181

Dear Mr. Gates:

John Miles recommended that I contact you about my interest in aviation law. Since I will be retiring from the U.S. Air Force next May, I am exploring career opportunities with companies interested in my expertise in aviation law. John said you were in the process of creating a new position dealing with structured settlements, an area in which I have had major responsibility when working at Headquarters in Washington, DC.

My legal experience with the Air Force includes the following duties, responsibilities, and accomplishments:

▪ <u>Chief Circuit Defense Counsel, Davis Air Force Base, Ogden, UT</u>: Personally defended all Flying Evaluation Boards (4), winning every one. Successfully defended felony trials covering offenses of drug use, distribution, assault, DUI, and perjury. Supervised, trained, and directed 22 attorneys and 17 paralegals responsible for total defense services across 16 Air Force installations located in 12 states. Included oversight of over 500 trials with every offense up to and including premeditated murder. 2002-present

▪ <u>Chief, Aviation Settlement Branch, U.S. Air Force, Washington, DC</u>: Directed the investigation, adjudication, and either settlement or litigation of all aviation, environmental, medical malpractice, and other tort claims filed against the Air Force. In 1994, this topped a $40 billion dollar exposure with the percentage of payout to claimed amount the lowest in over a decade. Supervised staff of 13 attorneys and 5 paralegals. Reformulated U.S. Air Force policy on tort claim and litigation matters in conjunction with the Department of Justice leading to a better concept and application of paying the losers and spending time and resources to win-the-winners. 1999-2001

▪ <u>Chief, Tort Section, U.S. Air Force, Washington, DC</u>: Supervised the investigation and recommended adjudication or litigation of all aviation tort claims against the Air Force, including the last of the Agent Orange cases and the KAL 007 Korean airliner shoot-down by the

Soviet Union. Supervised staff of 3 attorneys and 1 paralegal. Recommended U.S. Air Force policy change on aviation tort claims that directly resulted in greater Agency latitude for meritorious claims independent of the previously required GAO office requirements. 1995-1999

- Staff Judge Advocate, Stevens Air Force Base, Miami, FL: Advised top management of all legal issues to include the convening of Aircraft Accident Boards and Flying Evaluation Boards. Directed tort, labor, environmental, procurement, and criminal law procedures. During this period, defended two state environmental Notice of Violations successfully, and over 40 criminal cases were prosecuted without a single acquittal. Served as management's Chief Labor Resolution Negotiator securing settlements at 60 percent of the previously approved maximums. Supervised staff of 4 attorneys and 5 paralegals. 1991-1994

- Assistant Staff Judge Advocate, Lowry Air Force Base, CO: Served as government prosecutor for over 35 trials with no acquittals. Served as government representative in over 20 administrative hearings with no losses. Counseled clients on rights/duties under state and federal law. 1987-1990

- Area Defense Counsel, Marshall Air Force Base, Austin, TX: Defended over 300 clients in criminal trials, administrative hearings, or minor disciplinary concerns. 1984-1986

Please let me know if you need any additional information. I will call you next week concerning my interest in Boeing. I look forward to speaking with you.

Sincerely,

Steven Marsh

Steven Marsh

Broadcast
(International/Construction)

1131 N. Bridge Road
Baltimore, MD 21027

December 7, 20____

I am interested in an overseas construction management/supervision position with an international design/build firm. My experience includes:

- <u>Management</u>: Owner and President for 14 years of a design/build firm with annual revenues between $1 and $2 million.

- <u>Construction</u>: Direct experience with most methodologies of construction including wood frame, masonry, and light metal.

- <u>Supervision</u>: Responsible for 15 full-time employees. Concurrently supervised several hundred sub-contractors/crews. Many crews were non-English speaking.

- <u>Architectural design</u>: Residential experience with custom and tract family homes ranging from 1,000 to 10,000 square feet. Commercial experience with retail, office, office/warehouse, warehouse, restaurants, and marinas.

- <u>Overseas</u>: Fluent in German, written and spoken. Experienced working, researching, and residing abroad – 11 years in northern Europe and several Third World countries.

If my interests, skills, and experience coincide with your hiring needs, I would appreciate hearing from you. I can be contacted at 301-111-0981.

Sincerely,

George Willington

George Willington
<u>willingtong@trc.com</u>

9

Follow-Up Letters
That Get Action

YOUR LETTERS AND RESUMES are only as good as your follow-up methods. While the most efficient and effective follow-up method will be the telephone, on occasion you may want to write follow-up letters to be mailed, faxed, or e-mailed to your contacts. This normally occurs when you cannot get a phone number, or the letter recipient does not return your phone call after repeated attempts to contact them. These letters are initiated by you in an attempt to get the letter recipient to take action related to the content of your letter.

At the same time, you may write several follow-up letters in response to information received from or requests made by others. For example, your follow-up telephone call may result in a request to send samples of your work or to complete an application or other type of form. These follow-up letters are extremely important because you now have a foot, however tentative, in someone's door.

Whatever you do, treat these follow-up letters with tender loving care! They may be your ticket to the next step – a job interview.

Persistence Pays Off

Conducting a telephone follow-up is easier said than done. Many vacancy announcements purposefully avoid identifying their organization by name and telephone in order to avoid walk-ins and telephone calls. Even when you have a name and telephone number, many employers prefer not taking phone calls from applicants simply because they are not prepared to talk with you about a hiring decision and don't want to be forced into making a decision by an assertive applicant. They would rather you went away and waited for them to contact you. You may call several times and leave messages on voice mail, but no one returns your calls. If you talk to someone, it's likely to be a receptionist or other type of gatekeeper. You probably will be told by the gatekeeper that the individual you are calling for is *"on the other line," "in a meeting," "not available at this time,"* or *"she will get back with you later."* In many cases these are code words for not wanting to speak with you. A gatekeeper takes your name, phone number, and message, but you never receive a return call. After making three to five such unsuccessful follow-up calls, it's time to write a follow-up letter instead.

When to Write

The follow-up letters in this chapter serve as alternatives to the follow-up telephone call. If you have not received a reply to your initial letter within two weeks, it's safe to assume you will not be receiving a reply at all. Begin making your follow-up telephone calls after one week to ten days. If you cannot reach the individual by phone within three days, go ahead and write a follow-up letter. Waiting any longer will probably be a waste of time. E-mailing or faxing your letter should be more effective than sending it through the mail.

Control Your Enclosures and Emotions

The most effective follow-up letters should include two items – a copy of your original letter and mention of your telephone number for convenience in responding to you. If you are requesting information, you may want to include a self-addressed stamped envelope for convenience of the letter recipient.

If you are angry after making six follow-up telephone calls and getting no response (what jerks!), try not to express your disappointment or feelings in your follow-up letter. Keep your tone positive and upbeat. Persistence in a friendly and professional manner is more likely to pay off with a response.

Information Request

124 Linden Place
Chicago, IL 60002

October 15, 20____

Mindi Mason, Director
ENVIRONMENTAL RESEARCH
   CENTER
147 Gilbert Avenue
San Francisco, CA 91441

Dear Ms. Mason:

On October 2, I wrote to you requesting information on organizations involved in conducting environmental research on tropical rainforests. Since I have not heard from you, I assume you may not have received my original letter.

I enclose a copy of the original letter for your reference. I would appreciate whatever assistance you could give me. Should you need to call, I can be reached at 410-381-8214.

Sincerely,

Steven Wallace

Steven Wallace
wallaces@aol.com

Placement Services

853 West Norton Road
Boise, ID 88344

July 22, 20____

James Walters, Director
Information Services
ASSOCIATION OF
     AMERICAN ACCOUNTANTS
5391 Tyler Road
Washington, DC 20543

Dear Mr. Walters:

Did you receive the enclosed letter? I wrote it on July 8, but did not have your name at that time. Perhaps it was forwarded to the wrong person.

As I mentioned in my earlier letter, I would appreciate information on your placement or job search services. If you don't have such information, can you recommend any other organizations that might provide such assistance to accountants?

Should you want to contact me by phone, my number is 818-371-9821. I appreciate your assistance.

Sincerely,

George Miles

George Miles
milesg@aol.com

Alumni Network Information

973 West End
New York, NY 10001

March 10, 20____

Wanda Evans, Director
Alumni Services
UNIVERSITY OF
    SOUTHERN CALIFORNIA
1933 Jasper Street
Los Angeles, CA 90312

Dear Ms. Evans:

I am having difficulty getting information on the USC alumni group in Houston. As indicated in the enclosed copy of my letter to you on February 13, I would like to make contacts with fellow alumni concerning my interests in international investment banking.

Could you please let me know if you have such information? I tried calling your office several times but was told you were not available. I enclose a self-addressed stamped envelope for your convenience. My phone number is 317-892-9881.

I appreciate your assistance.

Sincerely,

Brenda Carpenter

Brenda Carpenter
carpenterb@erols.com

Placement Assistance

246 Cathedral Drive
Salt Lake City, UT 86732

July 15, 20_____

James Martin
Association Referral Service
U.S. CHAMBER OF COMMERCE
1615 H Street, NW
Washington, DC 20062

Dear Mr. Martin:

Did you get my letter of June 3? Assuming it got lost along the way, I enclose a copy of the original for your reference.

I am interested in receiving information on employment opportunities in Western Europe. For your convenience, I enclose a self-addressed stamped envelope. I also can be reached at Tel. 818-839-9193 or by email: vertimosas@ace.com.

Many thanks for your assistance.

Sincerely,

Sandra Vertimosa

Sandra Vertimosa
vertimosas@ace.com

Information on Company

4439 Center Street
Portland, OR 98211

February 20, 20____

Melaine Roberts, Director
Public Relations Office
TRC PHARMACEUTICAL COMPANY
1000 West Knight Street
Terre Haute, IN 48732

Dear Ms. Roberts:

Did you get my letter of January 30? I enclose a copy for reference as well as a self-addressed stamped envelope for your convenience.

As I mentioned in my earlier letter, I am conducting research on various pharmaceutical companies as part of a career development project. I would really appreciate information on TRC Pharmaceutical Company.

Thank you in advance for your assistance.

Sincerely,

Jeffrey Williams

Jeffrey Williams
williamsj@earthone.com

Relocation Services

9341 Capitol Street
Omaha, NE 54371
March 15, 20____

David Allison, Director
Relocation Department
CENTURY 21
9431 Sheridan Road
Austin, TX 77211

Dear Mr. Allison:

Thanks so much for your prompt reply to my letter of March 3 for information on housing in the Austin community. The maps, brochures, and other publications were most helpful in giving us a good overview of the Austin housing market.

Could you do us one more favor? Our daughter needs special education services for students with physical disabilities. Which schools would provide such services and how close are they to the neighborhoods you identified in your letter of March 7?

We look forward to hearing from you and meeting with you when we visit Austin next month.

Sincerely,

Janice Wilson

Janice Wilson
wilsonj@aol.com

Subscription and Referral Services

113 Bellflower Ct.
Orono, ME 08013

August 23, 20____

April Burgess
Subscription Manager
ACCESS: Networking in the
    Public Interest
50 Beacon Street
Boston, MA 02108

Dear Ms. Burgess:

Thanks so much for your prompt response to my letter of August 9 for subscription and referral services. I enclose a check for $30 to cover the four-month subscription to <u>Community Jobs</u>.

I would also like to take advantage of your job matching services for an additional $20. Therefore, I enclose a copy of my resume, a completed data form, and check to initiate my participation in this databank program.

I look forward to receiving my first issue of your publication.

Sincerely,

Stacey Chino

Stacey Chino
<u>chinos@ace.net</u>

Information and Employment Services

1134 Stanford Lane
Orlando, FL 31339

July 23, 20____

Janice Eaton
HIGH TEMPS
73 Weston Road
Suite 913
Orlando, FL 31341

Dear Ms. Eaton:

Thanks for sending me information on your temporary employment services. I completed and am returning the registration and background information form you sent me. I also enclose a copy of my resume which I have revised since sending it to you on July 11. Please replace the one you have on file with this "new improved" version.

I look forward to meeting you next Monday at 10:30am to discuss how my interests and experience might best meet the needs of your clients.

Sincerely,

Martin Davis

Martin Davis
davism@erols.com

Assessing Job Search Services

5431 Atlanta Blvd.
Atlanta, GA 33479

May 9, 20____

Thomas Allen
BH Careers International
848 Peachtree Plaza
Atlanta, GA 33481

Dear Mr. Allen:

Thank you for sending me information on your career counseling services. I have had a chance to review the sample contract you sent. I fully understand that you provide career counseling and job search services rather than job placement services. I believe this is exactly what I need at this stage of my job search.

Could we meet to further discuss my needs and how Bernard Haldane Associates would work with me over a two-month period? I have had a chance to visit your website: www.bhcareers.com. I'm still not clear about the actual process I would be involved in. Perhaps you could answer a few questions some friends have raised about contracting for such services. I've been told I can do all of this work on my own without hiring a firm such as yours. I'm still not sure I'm doing the right thing. Perhaps you could enlighten me on why it would be in my best interests to sign a contract with BH Careers International. I'm especially interested in learning what happened to others who have used your services.

Please let me know when we might be able to meet. My phone number is 717-293-1240.

Sincerely,

Paul Martinez

Paul Martinez
martinezp@aol.com

Information for Recruitment

752 Thompson Court
Albany, NY 14321

April 23, 20____

James Reston
HEALTH SYSTEMS RECRUITERS
918 Monroe Street
Chicago, IL 60021

Dear Mr. Reston:

Thank you for your letter of April 2, in which you requested I complete the enclosed Career Fact Sheet for your records. I appreciate your willingness to include me in your recruitment circle.

In response to your question concerning my availability for overseas assignments, my answer is both yes and no. Since I have worked abroad for more than six years, I have no problem operating in the international arena. Indeed, I have very much enjoyed my international work and look forward to continuing it in the near future. However, my personal situation – single mother – is such that I prefer short-term assignments rather than residence abroad. My two children will enter high school during the next two years. I believe it's important that they experience their high school years here in the States. My ideal situation would be to travel abroad on assignments for no more than six to eight weeks each year.

I look forward to working with you over the coming weeks. Please give me a call if you have any questions: 204-381-0991.

Sincerely,

Doris Luffert

Doris Luffert
luffertd@aol.com

Rejecting Employment Service

8801 West End St.
Cleveland, OH 45313

January 13, 20____

Rob Richards
JOBS ABROAD
203 Ocean Blvd.
Ft. Lauderdale, FL 31111

Dear Mr. Richards:

I appreciated your prompt reply to my inquiry of December 29 about jobs in Australia. However, I must decline your service. I understand you are asking me to send you a check for $165 so you can help me find a job in Australia.

I'll keep my $165. A friend told me they used a similar service that sent them a travel video and a 10-page listing of names and addresses he could have gotten by spending 10 minutes in the public library. In addition, I called the Better Business Bureau in Ft. Lauderdale and learned they never heard of you or your company. Therefore, I've decided not to take a chance on paying money for what could be another unpleasant experience reported by others who have used similar services.

Please do not share my name and address with other firms.

Sincerely,

Daryl Peterson

Daryl Peterson

Information Needs

THOMAS EVANS   evanst@aol.com

1901 Davis Road   Little Rock, AR 79831   719-319-4601

May 16, 20____

William Billings
Director of Training
MANAGEMENT TRAINERS INC.
319 Garner Street, Suite 130
Little Rock, AR 79831

Dear Mr. Billings:

Thank you for your letter of May 11 in response to my earlier inquiry concerning management training opportunities with MTI.

As you requested, I enclose copies of course outlines for the two most popular courses I teach:

- Program Evaluation
- Managing Effective Meetings

During the past three years I have instructed over 300 individuals in each of these courses. I also enclose a sampling of evaluation comments I've received from participants during the past six months.

As I mentioned earlier, I also have developed the course materials for each of these courses. Each trainee receives a 100+ page loose-leaf training manual as part of their course materials. The manual, which is designed to be self-directed, has become very popular with several organizations that now purchase it separately for employees who are unable to attend my three-day workshop. I think there is a good market here for additional training materials. Perhaps you would be interested in discussing how my work with training materials could potentially evolve into a profit center for MTI.

Please give me a call if you need any additional information. I look forward to meeting you soon to discuss our mutual interests.

Sincerely,

Thomas Evans

Thomas Evans

Request for More Information

2984 Independent Road
Wichita, KS 58722

April 29, 20____

Martha Williamson
MCR VIDEO PRODUCTIONS
8193 Center Street
Wichita, KS 58721

Dear Ms. Williamson:

Thank you for speaking with me today about your graphic art needs. As you requested, I enclose a sample video of my animation work.

I believe this video adequately represents my graphic art interests and skills. Most of this work was completed on an Aurora 240.

As I mentioned in my letter of April 19, Michael Thiel should be able to answer other questions you may have about my work.

I look forward to meeting you soon.

Sincerely,

Grace Olson

Grace Olson
olsong@cmo.com

Confirming Appointment

781 Lincoln Highway
Springfield, IL 62881
June 22, 20____

Peter Weston
ALLIED HEALTHCARE
913 West Finley Avenue
Springfield, IL 62876

Dear Mr. Weston:

I enjoyed speaking with you today about your vacancy for a Senior EDP Auditor. Yes, I am still interested in this position.

I look forward to meeting you next Thursday at 1:30pm to discuss how my interests and experience can best meet your accounting needs. If you don't mind, I will bring a sample of my work with me. I'm especially interested in sharing with you some changes I've made in the EDP Audit function which seem to work well in reducing accounting costs.

Sincerely,

Patricia Dooley

Patricia Dooley
dooleyp@aol.com

Job Inquiry

SHELTON HULL   hulls@erols.com

159 Grand Avenue   Lincoln, NE 58271   713-820-6615

September 25, 20____

Julia Warner, Principal
LINCOLN HIGH SCHOOL
829 Main Street
Lincoln, NE 58270

Dear Ms. Warner:

Last January I wrote to you inquiring about possible vacancies for Social Science teachers. When I spoke to you over the phone, you indicated you were under a hiring freeze due to budgetary cuts affecting your staffing levels.

I enclose a copy of my newly revised resume for your reference. It reflects additional teaching experience and training I received during this past year.

Please keep me in mind should your hiring needs change. Hopefully we will be seeing fewer budgetary freezes for education this coming year!

Sincerely,

Shelton Hull

Shelton Hull

Vacancy Announcement

136 West Davis St.
Sacramento, CA 98771

September 15, 20____

Vicki Beatress
S.R. SYSTEMS
893 Mountain View Road
Sacramento, CA 98777

Dear Ms. Beatress:

On September 5, I sent you a copy of the attached letter in application for a Sales Associate position. Have you had a chance to make any preliminary decisions?

I want to reiterate my interest in this position and availability for an interview. I believe my interests, skills, and experience are an excellent fit for this position.

I will call you next Thursday to answer any questions you may have about my candidacy.

Sincerely,

Wayne Watson

Wayne Watson
watsonw@aol.com

Interview Confirmation

1234 Main Street
Norfolk, VA 23508

April 30, 20_____

Dale Roberts
Business Manager
VIRGINIA BEACH
   CONVENTION CENTER
2981 Ocean Boulevard
Virginia Beach, VA 23519

Dear Mr. Roberts:

Just a quick note to reconfirm our appointment next Tuesday at 10:30am. I look forward to discussing with you how my interests, skills, and experience can promote the Virginia Beach Convention Center.

As you requested, I enclose a copy of my resume for your reference. Please let me know if you need any additional information before our meeting on Tuesday.

Sincerely,

Karen Jones

Karen Jones
karenjones@earthone.com

Vacancy Announcement

MONIQUE ATLER   atlerm@ace.com

2589 Jason Drive   Ithaca, NY 14850   208-467-8735

April 27, 20___

Robert Byers
LAW ENFORCEMENT INSTITUTE
9881 Erie Road, Suite 203
Buffalo, NY 15283

Dear Mr. Byers:

When I called your office today, I learned you would be out of town until next Thursday. I was calling in reference to my letter of April 20 in which I inquired about an impending research, data analysis, and planning position.

I will call you again next Friday to discuss my continuing interest in working with the Law Enforcement Institute.

Sincerely,

Monique Atler

Monique Atler

Vacancy Announcement

997 Mountain Road
Denver, CO 80222

June 11, 20____

James Fountain
SIMON WALTERS, INC.
771 George Washington Blvd.
Denver, CO 80220

Dear Mr. Fountain:

I'm not doing well in the telephone department. I called your office several times yesterday but was unable to get through to you. After my sixth try, I decided Thursday was one of your incredibly busy days. And you really didn't need another phone call to top off your day!

I was just following up on my letter of June 4 in application for the bookkeeper position you had advertised in last week's <u>Rocky Mountain Times</u>. Have you had a chance to review my application? I also wanted to let you know that I am still interested in this position and would appreciate an opportunity to meet with you to discuss how my interests, skills, and experience can best contribute to sound financial reporting at Simon Walters, Inc.

I'll try to call you again next Tuesday. Perhaps your schedule will be less hectic by that time.

Sincerely,

Jane Barrows

Jane Barrows
<u>barrowsj@erols.com</u>

Vacancy Announcement

ROBBIN BARRETT   barrettr@skyweb.com
221 Western Ave.   Detroit, MI 47892   919-231-3214

November 13, 20_____

Katherine Kerry
Recruitment Director
CONSUMER UNION
29 Temple Place
Boston, MA 02111

Dear Ms. Kerry:

Thank you for speaking with me today concerning my application for the Consumer Program Associate position. Your description of the position better clarified my understanding of how this position fits into the larger operations of the Consumer Union.

I want to reiterate my continuing interest in this position. Indeed, after learning the position will involve creating new citizen outreach offices – something I've been very active and successful in doing for the past three years – I'm more interested than ever in working with the Consumer Union. This is the type of grassroots activity I most enjoy. It's also a good organizational strategy for building the networks necessary for mobilizing public support behind Consumer Union's environmental protection efforts.

Please let me know if you need any additional information about my candidacy. I look forward to meeting you in the very near future to discuss how I see this position evolving both within Consumer Union and at the community level.

Sincerely,

Robbin Barrett

Robbin Barrett

Vacancy Announcement

712 W. Vermont St.
Washington, DC 20132
May 9, 20____

Elliott Stevens
WASHINGTON MONTHLY
1611 Connecticut Avenue, NW
Washington, DC 20009

Dear Mr. Stevens:

Just a quick note to clarify my continuing interest in the Summer Circulation Intern position I applied for on May 3. As I discussed with you over the phone today, I was not sure whether I wanted to intern on a part-time or full-time basis this summer. Please don't get me wrong. I don't mean to appear indecisive or disinterested. I just didn't think about the possibility that this would be a full-time position. For some reason I was led to believe, based upon conversations with other classmates who have interned, that most Summer Internship positions were part-time. Now I know better.

After talking with you, I decided to set some priorities in relation to this position and my career interests. What I really want is a full-time position. I think I will both contribute and learn the most by interning on a full-time basis during the next three months.

Will you be scheduling interviews for this position soon? I would appreciate the opportunity to further discuss how my interests and skills could be best used in this position.

Sincerely,

Tracey Nelson

Tracey Nelson
nelsont@aol.com

Vacancy Announcement

2908 Trail Drive
Atlanta, GA 32119

October 9, 20____

Barbara Haynes
Department of Dispute Resolution
SUPREME COURT OF GEORGIA
100 N. Eighth Street, 2nd Floor
Atlanta, GA 32109

Dear Ms. Haynes:

Thanks so much for taking time from your busy schedule to discuss my application for the position of Dispute Resolution Intake Coordinator in DeKalb County.

I agree with you that this position should involve a major grantsmanship component. New federal monies are now available through the Department of Justice to fund experimental dispute resolution programs. I'm also aware of a little known grant program in the Department of Housing and Urban Development for mediating jurisdictional disputes within urban counties. And I believe a new Cooperative Agreement program dealing with mediation programs will be announced through the Department of Justice within the next six months. The new Dispute Resolution Intake Coordinator should explore these and other programs for DeKalb County.

I appreciated your time in discussing this position and your program. As I indicated in my letter of September 29, I have a strong interest in this position and working with your organization. This is one of the most innovative programs I have encountered anywhere in the country. It deserves a Dispute Resolution Intake Coordinator who has the necessary entrepreneurial skills to sustain and expand a successful program.

I would appreciate an opportunity to meet with you about this position. I have several other ideas I would like to share with you on grantsmanship skills appropriate for the position. Should you have any questions, my number is 313-781-9831.

Sincerely,

Kevin Anderson

Kevin Anderson
andersonk@trc.com

Vacancy Announcement

WANDA PETERS, RN
213 Padra Fara, Apt. 137
Manila, The Philippines
Tel. 011-82-283-447
Fax 011-82-283-292
petersw@philword.com

June 27, 20____

Doris Silverman, MS, RN
Nurse Recruiter
OREGON GENERAL REHAB CENTER
8187 Elkins Drive
Portland, OR 98309

Dear Ms. Silverman:

As a follow-up to my June 23 letter of application for the Rehab Nurse position, I wanted to let you know that my schedule for returning to the States is now final. I will arrive in Portland on July 17. Assuming the position may still be vacant, could we meet sometime during the week of July 19 to discuss my candidacy?

I will call your office as soon as I arrive in Portland to see if your schedule would permit such a meeting.

Sincerely,

Wanda Peters

Wanda Peters, RN

Vacancy Announcement

717 Georgia Avenue
Indianapolis, IN 48712

March 9, 20_____

Barry Bates
Human Resources
GREATER INDIANAPOLIS HOSPITAL
67100 Conners Road
Indianapolis, IN 48712

Dear Mr. Bates:

Thanks so much for returning my call today. I appreciated your thoughtfulness and learned a great deal about your needs and the nature of the
Occupational Therapist position.

As you requested, I instructed my university placement office to send you a
copy of my file. It includes transcripts, three letters of recommendation,
and a sample of my work. Since I requested these documents be sent to
you by Federal Express, they should reach you within two days.

I'll give you a call next week to answer any additional questions you may
have about my interest in this position.

Sincerely,

Susan Wright

Susan Wright
wrights@aol.com

10

Thank You Letters –
A Powerful Personal Touch

THANK YOU LETTERS ARE SOME of the most powerful job search letters you will ever write. If you are like many other job seekers, your thank you letters may be more effective than your resume and cover letters. One well written and timed thank you letter may become the key to being invited to an interview or offered the job.

Get Remembered As Thoughtful

Why are short, simple, and superficial thank you letters so effective in a job search – especially when compared to lengthier job search letters and resumes?

Thank you letters demonstrate an important **social grace** that says something about you as an individual – your personality and how you probably relate to others. They communicate an important characteristic sought by many employers – **thoughtfulness**.

Better still, since few individuals write thank you letters, those who do write them are **remembered** by letter recipients. And one thing you definitely want to happen again and again during your job search is to be remembered by individuals who can provide you with useful information, advice, and referrals as well as invite you to job interviews and extend to you job offers. For being remembered as a thoughtful person with the proper social graces will give you **an edge** over many other job seekers who fail to write thank you letters. Whatever you do, make sure you regularly send thank you letters in response to individuals who assist you in your job search.

Many job seekers discover the most important letters they ever wrote were thank you letters. These letters can have several positive outcomes:

■ **Contacts turn into more contacts and job interviews:** A job seeker sends a thank you letter to someone who recommended she contact a former college roommate; impressed with the thoughtfulness of the job seeker and feeling somewhat responsible for helping her make the right contacts, the individual continues providing additional referrals, which eventually lead to two job interviews.

■ **Job interview turns into a job offer:** A job seeker completes a job interview. Within 24 hours he writes a nice thank you letter expressing his gratitude for having an opportunity to interview for the position as well as reiterates his interest in working for the employer. This individual is subsequently offered the job. The employer later tells him it was his thoughtful thank you letter that gave him the edge over two other equally qualified candidates who never bothered to follow up.

> *Being remembered as a thoughtful person will give you an edge over many other job seekers.*

■ **A job rejection later turns into a job offer:** After interviewing for a position, a job seeker receives a standard rejection letter from an employer indicating the job was offered to another individual. Rather than get angry and end communications, the job seeker sends a nice thank you letter in which she notes her disappointment in not being selected and then thanks him for the opportunity to interview for the position. She also reiterates her continuing interest in the organization. The employer remembers this individual. Rather than let her get away, he decides to create a new position for her.

■ **A job offer turns into an immediate positive relationship:** Upon receiving a job offer, the new employee sends a nice thank you letter in which he expresses his appreciation for the confidence expressed by the employer. He also reassures the employer that he will be as productive as expected. This letter is well received by the employer, who is looking forward to working closely with such a thoughtful new employee. Indeed, he becomes a mentor and sponsor who immediately gives the employee some plum assignments that help him fast-track his career within the organization.

- **Termination results in strong recommendations and a future job offer:** An employee, seeking to advance her career with a larger organization, receives a job offer from a competing firm. In submitting her formal letter of resignation, she also sends a personal thank you letter to her former employer. She sincerely expresses her gratitude for having the opportunity to work with him and attributes much of her success to his mentoring. This letter further confirms his conclusion about this former employee – he's losing a valuable asset. While he cannot offer her a similar or better career opportunity in this organization, he will keep her in mind if things change. And things do change two years later when he makes a major career move to a much larger organization. One of the first things he does as Vice President is to begin shaping his own personal staff. He immediately contacts her to see if she would be interested in working with him. She's interested and soon joins her former employer in making another major career move.

In these cases it was the job seekers' thank you letters, rather than their cover letters and resumes, that gave them the edge and landed them job interviews.

As indicated in the above scenarios, thank you letters should be written in the following situations:

- **After receiving information, advice, or a referral from a contact:** You should always express your gratitude in writing to individuals who provide you with job search assistance. Not only is this a nice thing to do, it also is functional for a successful job search. Individuals who feel they are appreciated will most likely remember you and be willing to further assist you with your job search and recommend you to others.

- **Immediately after interviewing for a job:** Whether it be a telephone or face-to-face interview, always write a nice thank you letter within 12 hours of completing the interview. This letter should express your gratitude for having an opportunity to interview for the job. Be sure to reiterate your interest in the job and stress your possible contributions to the employer's operations. The letter should emphasize some of your major strengths in relationship to the employer's needs. All other things being equal, this letter may give you an "extra edge" over other candidates. It may well prove to be the most effective letter in your entire job search!

- **Withdrawing from further consideration:** At some point during the recruitment process, you may decide to withdraw from further consideration. Perhaps you decided to take another job, you're now more satisfied with your present job, or the position no longer interests you. For whatever reason, you should write a short thank you letter in which you withdraw from consideration. Explain in positive terms why you are no longer interested in pursuing an application with the organization. Thank them for their time and consideration.

- **After receiving a rejection:** Even if you receive a rejection, it's a good idea to write a thank you letter. How many employers ever receive such a letter from what ostensibly should be a disappointed job seeker? This unique letter is likely to be remembered – which is what you want to accomplish in this situation. Being remembered may result in referrals to other employers or perhaps a job interview and offer at some later date.

- **After receiving a job offer:** However well they think they hire, employers still are uncertain about the outcome of their hiring decisions until new employees perform in their organization. Why not put their initial anxieties at ease and get off on the right foot by writing a nice thank you letter? In this letter express your appreciation for having received the confidence and trust of the employer. Reiterate what you told the employer during the job interview(s) about your goals and expected performance. Conclude with a reaffirmation of your starting date as well as a statement about how much you look forward to becoming a productive member of the team. Such a thoughtful letter will be well received by the employer. It could well accelerate your progress within the organization beyond the norm.

- **Upon leaving a job:** Whether you leave your job voluntarily or are forced by circumstances to terminate, try to leave a positive part of you behind by writing a thank you letter. Burning bridges behind you through face-to-face confrontation or a vindictive, get-even letter may later catch up with you, especially if you anger someone in the process who may later be in a position to affect your career. If you quit to take a job with another organization, thank your employer for the time you spent with the organization and the opportunities given to you to acquire valuable experience and skills.

If you terminated under difficult circumstances – organizational cutbacks or a nasty firing – try to leave on as positive a note as possible. Employers in such situations would rather have you out of sight and mind. Assure them there are no hard feelings, and you wish them the best as you would hope they would wish you the same. Stress the positives of your relationship with both the employer and the organization. Remember, your future employer may call your previous employer for information on your past performance. If you leave a stressful situation on a positive note, chances are your previous employer will give you the benefit of the doubt and stress only your positives to others. He may even commit a few "sins of omission" that only you and he know about: *"She really worked well with her co-workers and was one of our best analysts"* does not tell the whole story which may be that you couldn't get along with your boss, and vice versa. After having made peace with each other through the medium of the thank you letter, what would your former employer have to gain by telling the whole story to others about your work with him? Your thank you letter should at least neutralize the situation and at best turn a negative situation into a positive for your career. Indeed, he may well become one of your supporters – for other jobs with other employers, that is!

The remainder of this chapter presents examples of each type of letter, written according to our principles of effective thank you letters.

Thank you letters should always be written in a timely manner. Make it a practice to sit down and write these letters within 12 hours of the situation that prompts this letter. It should be mailed immediately so that it reaches the recipient within three to four days. If you wait longer, the letter will have less impact on the situation. Indeed, in the case of the interview thank you letter, if an employer is making a final hiring decision among three candidates, your letter should arrive as soon as possible to have a chance to affect the outcome.

Whether you handwrite or type this letter may not make a great deal of difference in terms of outcomes, but your choice says something about your professional style and mentality. Many people claim handwritten thank you letters are more powerful than typed letters. We doubt such claims and have yet to see any credible data on the subject other than personal preferences and questionable logic. It is true that handwritten thank you letters communicate a certain personal element that cannot be expressed in typewritten letters. If you choose to handwrite this letter, make sure you have attractive handwriting. Your handwriting form and style could be a negative.

The problem with handwritten letters is that they can express a certain nonprofessional, amateurish style. They also may raise questions about your motivations and manipulative style. They turn off some readers who expect a business letter, rather than an expression of social graces, in reference to a business situation. Furthermore, some readers may consider the handwritten letter an attempt at psychological manipulation – they know what you're trying to do by handwriting a letter. That's what real estate and car salespeople are taught to do in their training seminars! When in doubt, it's best to type this letter in a neat, clean, and professional manner. If typewritten, such a personal letter also will express your professional style and respond to the expectations appropriate for the situation. It tells the reader that you know proper business etiquette, you know this is a business situation, you are equipped to respond, and you attempt to demonstrate your best professional effort.

Post Informational Interview

9910 Thompson Drive
Cleveland, OH 43382

June 21, 20____

Jane Evans, Director
EVANS FINANCE CORPORATION
2122 Forman Street
Cleveland, OH 43380

Dear Ms. Evans:

Your advice was most helpful in clarifying my questions on careers in finance. I am now reworking my resume and have included many of your thoughtful suggestions. I will send you a copy next week.

Thanks so much for taking time from your busy schedule to see me. I will keep in contact and follow through on your suggestion to see Sarah Cook about opportunities with the Cleveland-Akron Finance Company.

Sincerely,

Daryl Haines

Daryl Haines
hainesd@aol.com

Post Informational Interview

9855 Little Glen Court
Dallas, TX 75207

July 29, 20____

Ida Stonewall
PACIFIC DESIGN CENTER
7008 Melrose Avenue
Los Angeles, CA 90069

Dear Ms. Stonewall:

Thank you for taking the time to meet with me yesterday. I thoroughly enjoyed our meeting, and the information you gave me was most helpful.

I have already contacted three of the people you suggested I should talk with and have appointments to meet with them over the next two weeks. The fourth person, Jerrie Forsythe, is on vacation so I will try to contact her again next week.

I would appreciate it if you would keep me in mind if you talk with someone in the near future who is looking for an individual with credentials similar to mine. Talking with you only made me more anxious to get into a job in a design center.

As you suggested, I will keep in touch with you over the next few weeks and let you know how my job search is going.

Most sincerely,

JoAnne McGrosney

JoAnne McGrosney
joannemcg@earthone.net

Post Informational Interview

4183 Waupelani Drive
State College, PA 16808

December 1, 20____

Dr. Harold Selnik
Chairman
Department of Speech Communication
UNIVERSITY OF PITTSBURGH
Pittsburgh, PA 12511

Dear Dr. Selnik:

Thank you for taking the time to meet with me last Friday. It was most kind of you – especially since you took time from your Thanksgiving break at the university to do so. I found the meeting even more helpful to me than I had anticipated. I had never even considered some of the options open to someone with my major!

I have taken your advice and have made appointments to talk with some of the people whom you suggested. I am sure their advice will also be useful to me.

I will keep in touch with you and let you know what decisions I make and what opportunities I take during the remainder of this year.

Thanks again for helping me make some decisions very important to my future.

Sincerely,

Julie McGuire

Julie McGuire
mcguirej@ace.com

Post Informational Interview

921 West Fifth Street
Denver, CO 72105

July 18, 20_____

James R. Taylor
Assistant Manager
ASSOCIATED FINANCIAL
   ADVISORS
241 Skyline Road
Denver, CO 71088

Dear Mr. Taylor:

Joan Karvin was right when she said you would be most helpful in
advising me on a career in finance.

I appreciated your taking time from your busy schedule to meet with
me. Your advice was most helpful, and I have incorporated your suggestions into my resume. I will send you a copy next week.

Again, thanks so much for your assistance. As you suggested, I will
contact Mr. David James next week in regards to a possible opening with
his company.

Sincerely,

John Perkins

John Perkins
perkinsj@planetone.net

Post Informational Interview

4563 Southshore Drive
Key Biscayne, FL 33455

May 5, 20____

Marlo Sikes
Public Relations Director
DOLPHIN CRUISE LINE
873 North American Way
Miami, FL 33132

Dear Ms. Sikes:

I am grateful for the opportunity to meet with you today. As Mr. Barnes had indicated, you are certainly one of the best informed persons in the Miami area when it comes to questions about the cruise industry. Your knowledge as well as analysis of future trends is right on the mark, yet I had not looked at it that way before.

My discussion with you helped me focus on the direction I want to pursue. I really believe I would be happier working in a cruiseline's corporate offices rather than taking a job on board ship. You mentioned during our discussion that you would be happy to put me in contact with several people in your network if I decided this was the direction I wished to take.

I am writing to ask your assistance in making contact with these people. I will call you in a few days to get these names and addresses from you. I certainly appreciate this additional assistance on your part.

Thank you again for taking time from your busy schedule to meet with me. I look forward to seeing you again in the future – hopefully when I am working for a cruise line!

Sincerely,

Miriam Jordan

Miriam Jordan
jordanm@aol.com

Post Job Interview

2962 Forrest Drive
Denver, CO 82171

May 28, 20____

Thomas F. Harris
Director, Personnel Department
COASTAL PRODUCTS, INC.
7229 Lakewood Drive
Denver, CO 82170

Dear Mr. Harris:

Thank you again for the opportunity to interview for the marketing position. I appreciated your hospitality and enjoyed meeting you and members of your staff.

The interview convinced me of how compatible my background, interests, and skills are with the goals of Coastal Products Incorporated. My prior marketing experience with the Department of Commerce has prepared me to take a major role in developing both domestic and international marketing strategies. I am confident my work could result in increased market shares for Coastal Products Incorporated in the rapidly expanding Pacific Rim market.

For more information on the new product promotion program I mentioned, call David Garrett at the Department of Commerce; his number is 202-726-0132. I talked to Dave this morning and mentioned your interest in this program.

I look forward to meeting you and your staff again.

Sincerely,

Stephanie Potter

Stephanie Potter
potters@aol.com

Post Job Interview

1947 Grace Avenue
Springfield, MA 01281

November 17, 20____

James R. Quinn, Director
Personnel Department
DAVIS ENTERPRISES
2290 Cambridge Street
Boston, MA 01181

Dear Mr. Quinn:

Thank you for the opportunity to interview yesterday for the Sales Trainee position. I enjoyed meeting you and learning more about Davis Enterprises. You have a fine staff and a sophisticated approach to marketing.

Your organization appears to be growing in a direction which parallels my interests and career goals. The interview with you and your staff confirmed my initial positive impressions of Davis Enterprises, and I want to reiterate my strong interest in working for you. My prior experience in operating office equipment plus my training in communication would enable me to progress steadily through your training program and become a productive member of your sales team.

Again, thank you for your consideration. If you need any additional information from me, please feel free to call.

Yours truly,

Gail S. Topper

Gail S. Topper
topperg@aol.com

Post Job Interview

8712 Graham Blvd.
Staunton, VA 23212
January 28, 20____

Edward Jason
Personnel Administrator
CITY OF CHARLESTON
P.O. Box 4561
Charleston, WV 25331

Dear Mr. Jason:

I appreciated the opportunity to interview with you today. Having talked with you and found out in greater depth about the opening you have, I am more sure than ever that I would like to work for the City of Charleston as Parks and Recreation Director.

Having directed all phases of community recreational programs while I was the director in Staunton, I feel certain I could bring the kind of leadership to the program in Charleston that you indicate you need. I also feel certain that under my supervision it would be possible to expand the programs without the need to increase the budget. In these recessionary times that becomes a critical consideration.

I hope to have the opportunity to help Charleston revitalize its recreational programs. Please let me know if I may provide any further information that will be helpful as you make your hiring decision.

I will call you next Friday, as you suggested, to see how your selection process is going.

Sincerely,

Sylvia Whitehurst

Sylvia Whitehurst
whitehursts@ace.com

Post Job Interview

882 Forest Lane
Cleveland, OH 43210

March 16, 20____

Jonathan Morrison
Circulation Department
CLEVELAND PLAIN DEALER
8250 Lakefront Blvd.
Cleveland, OH 43208

Dear Mr. Morrison:

I really appreciated having the opportunity to interview with you today for the position of Dispatcher. I remain extremely interested in this position. I am especially interested because it is an evening job. I am used to working an evening schedule and feel I might have trouble adapting to a day job.

If I have not heard from you by next Friday, I will check back with you to see how your selection process is progressing. I look forward to hearing from you and hope I will have the opportunity to work with you.

Sincerely,

Jack Diamond

Jack Diamond
diamondj@aol.com

Post Job Interview

5680 Citrine Blvd.
Pekin, IL 61559

March 12, 20____

John Dingle
General Manager
PEORIA GAZETTE
13 Walsh Street
Peoria, IL 61564

Dear Mr. Dingle:

I wish to thank you for taking the time to meet with me yesterday. I enjoyed talking with you and finding out more about what is happening at the Peoria Gazette.

I found it fascinating that you are planning to innovate in areas similar to those where we at the Times have made recent changes. I believe I have a lot to offer to the Gazette and ask that you seriously consider me if you decide to restructure and add the new position in Personnel that we talked about. I met several interesting people at lunch with you yesterday and I know I would enjoy working with you and your staff.

I enclose the resume I promised to send you. I will call you in a few days to see whether you have any further questions.

Sincerely,

Jack Fielding

Jack Fielding
fieldingj@aol.com

Referral

5491 Mountain View Dr.
Sacramento, CA 95421

July 28, 20____

Martha Albertson
Personnel Department
HOLIDAY INN NATIONAL
319 Granite Stone Dr.
San Diego, CA 92351

Dear Ms. Albertson:

Sorry my letter in response to your ad in the <u>San Diego Times</u> arrived too late for me to be considered for the position. It certainly was kind of you to take time to suggest that I contact Dorothy Wiggins of Inn Tonight.

I have talked with Miss Wiggins and, although she does not have an opening I might fit at present, she indicated if I would send her a resume she would keep it on file.

I am writing to ask that you do the same. I am still very much interested in Holiday Inn National and hope that you will consider me for the next opening you may have. I enclose an additional copy of my resume for your information. My broad experience in guest services management would make me an ideal addition to your team.

I will hope to hear from you and will be in touch with you the next time I am in San Diego in about a month.

Sincerely,

Arthur Brenner

Arthur Brenner
<u>arthurbrenner@starweb.com</u>

Referral

485 High Bluff Road
Santa Fe, NM 89543

November 16, 20____

Rebecca Lyons
WESTERN INDUSTRIES, INC.
98347 W. Main Street
Albuquerque, NM 89977

Dear Mrs. Lyons:

I want to thank you for the referral you gave me. At your suggestion I contacted Deborah Johnson at Southwestern Products. The timing was perfect. They had an opening, and I was interviewed and offered the job. I will be starting there next week!

The job will be a promotion of sorts for me as well, since I will be the executive secretary to the vice president of operations. I look forward to my work there.

Sincerely,

Karen Jostney

Karen Jostney
jostneyk@aol.com

Referral

9821 West Fulton Street
Miami, FL 30303

March 7, 20____

Martin Davis
213 Doreen Drive
Miami, FL 30301

Dear Martin,

Thanks so much for putting me in contact with Jane Burton at Fordham Manufacturing Company.

I spoke with her today about my interests in technical training. She was most gracious with her time and provided me with a great deal of useful information on job opportunities in the Miami area. She even made some valuable suggestions for strengthening my resume and gave me a few names of individuals who might be interested in my qualifications.

I'll send you a copy of my resume once I revise it. Please feel free to make any comments or suggestions as well as share it with others who might be interested in my background.

Again, thanks so much for putting me in contact with Jane Burton. She spoke very highly of you and your work with the United Fund.

Sincerely,

Steven Zolbert

Steven Zolbert
zolberts@erols.com

Responding to Rejection

1947 Grace Avenue
Springfield, MA 01281

September 14, 20____

Sharon T. Avery
Vice President for Sales
BENTLEY ENTERPRISES
529 W. Sheridan Road
Washington, DC 20011

Dear Ms. Avery:

Thank you for giving me the opportunity to interview for the Customer Services Representative position. I appreciate your consideration and interest in me. I learned a great deal from our meetings.

Although I am disappointed in not being selected for your current vacancy, I want you to know that I appreciated the courtesy and professionalism shown to me during the entire selection process. I enjoyed meeting you, John Roberts, and other members of your sales staff. My meetings confirmed that Bentley Enterprises would be an exciting place to work and build a career.

I want to reiterate my strong interest in working for you. Please keep me in mind should another position become available in the near future.

Again, thank you for the opportunity to interview. Best wishes to you and your staff.

Yours truly,

Gail S. Topper

Gail S. Topper
topperg@aol.com

Responding to Rejection

455 Los Altos Drive
Los Angeles, CA 91095

October 24, 20____

Jennifer Strong
THE GREEN BEAN CO.
241 Greenbrier Road
Los Angeles, CA 91093

Dear Mrs. Strong:

I was sorry to hear of the selection of another candidate to fill the slot of manager of the first of three stores you will be opening in the L.A. area. However, I am certain that you had good reasons for the choice you made. My disappointment at not having been selected is someone else's joy.

I know you plan to open two more stores in this area over the next few months. I am writing to request that you keep my resume in an "open" file and reconsider my application for the two other slots as they become available. In fact, I enclose an additional copy of my resume for your convenience.

I have a high regard for your products, think my experience could serve you well, and hope to have the opportunity to talk with you again regarding future openings you will have in the L.A. area.

Thank you for your consideration.

Sincerely,

Linda Perry

Linda Perry
lindaperry@earthstar.com

Withdrawing From Consideration

4458 Enfield Drive
Norfolk, VA 23506

September 30, 20____

Jeffrey Allen
JEFFERSON MORTGAGE
   COMPANY
1873 Granby Street
Norfolk, VA 23500

Dear Mr. Allen:

On September 16th, I sent a cover letter and resume to you in response to your advertisement for a loan officer. Since I have not heard from you, I do not know whether my application is presently under consideration.

However, since I have just accepted a position with the Bank of Commerce, I am writing to request that you withdraw my application from consideration.

I have a high regard for your institution that has remained financially strong as a result of conservative lending practices. Perhaps our paths will cross and we will have the opportunity to meet in the future.

Sincerely,

Wanda Wright

Wanda Wright
wrightw@aol.com

Withdrawing From Consideration

3773 Nevada Street
Portland, OR 98677
July 5, 20____

Ann Jenkins
KALIN'S DRESS SHOP
3456 Centre Street
Portland, OR 98678

Dear Mrs. Jenkins:

Thank you for giving me the opportunity to talk with you yesterday about the opening you have for a salesperson at your store.

You were more helpful than you know. I had always thought working in a dress shop would be fun – the chance to work with all those pretty clothes! After talking with you, I realize how much hard work is involved before the clothing makes its way to the racks in the store. I no longer believe this is the right line of work for me. Thank you for helping me make an important decision.

You have a beautiful store and I have no doubt you will have no difficulty finding the right person to fill your sales opening.

Sincerely,

Angelique Martin

Angelique Martin
angeliquem@erols.com

Withdrawing From Consideration

2345 Glen Echo Court
Berea, OH 44375

October 7, 20____

Dr. Harriet Learner, Chair
Department of Communication
CUYAHOGA COMMUNITY COLLEGE
Cleveland, OH 44452

Dear Dr. Learner:

Thank you for selecting me to interview for the instructor position open
in the Communication Department for the coming academic year. I
appreciated the opportunity to meet with you and other members of the
faculty. You have an outstanding program and it would be a privilege for
me to have the opportunity to work with you.

However, I must request that you withdraw my application from further
consideration. I have just received an offer from the Leeward Community
College in Pearl City, Hawaii, to teach in their Department of Speech
Communication. This position will give me the chance to further my study
of the linguistic components of Native American speech; I hope to be able
to complete the book I am writing within the year.

I know you will have no trouble selecting a competent candidate to fill
your opening. I do plan to return to Ohio within a year or two to be
closer to my parents, and I hope we may be able to get together again at
that time. If you have an opening next year in my areas of specialty, I
would very much appreciate hearing about it at that time.

I will keep in touch with you over the next year.

Sincerely,

Marcus McDonald

Marcus McDonald
mcdonaldm@aol.com

Withdrawing From Consideration

733 Main Street
Williamsburg, VA 23512

December 1, 20____

Dr. Thomas C. Bostelli, President
NORTHERN STATES UNIVERSITY
2500 University Drive
Greenfield, MA 03241

Dear Dr. Bostelli:

It was indeed a pleasure meeting with you and your staff last week to discuss your need for a Director of Public and Government Relations. Our time together was most enjoyable and informative.

As I discussed with you during our meetings, I believe one purpose of preliminary interviews is to explore areas of mutual interest and to assess the fit between the individual and the position. After careful consideration, I have decided to withdraw from consideration for the position.

My decision is based upon several factors. First, the emphasis on fund raising is certainly needed, but I would prefer more balance in my work activities. Second, the position would require more travel than I am willing to accept with my other responsibilities. Third, professional opportunities for my husband would be very limited in northwest Massachusetts.

I want to thank you for interviewing me and giving me the opportunity to learn about your needs. You have a fine staff and faculty, and I would have enjoyed working with them.

Best wishes in your search.

Sincerely,

Janet L. Lawson

Janet L. Lawson
lawsonj@aol.com

Accepting Job Offer

2589 Jason Drive
Ithaca, NY 14850

August 19, 20

Sharon A. Waters
Personnel Director
NEW YORK STATE POLICE
Administrative Division
892 South Park
Albany, NY 11081

Dear Ms. Waters:

I want to thank you and Mr. Gordon for giving me the opportunity to work with the New York State Police. I am very pleased to accept the position as a research and data analyst with your planning unit. The position requires exactly the kind of work I want to do, and I know that I will do a good job for you.

As we discussed, I shall begin work on October 1. In the meantime, I shall compete all the necessary employment forms, obtain the required physical examination, and locate housing. I plan to be in Albany within the next two weeks and would like to deliver the paperwork to you personally. At that time we could handle any remaining items pertaining to my
employment. I'll call next week to schedule an appointment with you.

I enjoyed my interviews with you and Mr. Gordon and look forward to beginning my job with the Planning Unit.

Sincerely,

Cheryl Ayers

Cheryl Ayers
ayersc@ace.net

cc: Mr. Edward Gordon, Administrator
    Planning Unit

Accepting Job Offer

8172 Western Avenue
Cedar Rapids, IA 54019

September 29, 20____

Morris Edelson
ICRW INTERNATIONAL
28 W. 32nd Street
New York, NY 10031

Dear Mr. Edelson:

I was so pleased to receive the job offer from ICRW. I am appreciative of the confidence you have in my work and I will work hard to deserve the support you are giving me. I don't know which I am more excited about – the work I will be doing or the location where I will be working. The chance to work on-site in Indonesia will be extremely interesting.

I look forward to working with you and the staff of ICRW over the coming year.

Sincerely,

Lynne Gardner

Lynne Gardner
gardnerlyn@aol.com

Accepting Job Offer

712 W. Vermont St.
Washington, DC 20132

June 10, 20____

Elliott Stevens
WASHINGTON MONTHLY
1611 Connecticut Ave., NW
Washington, DC 20009

Dear Mr. Stevens:

It is with great anticipation that I accept your offer of a summer internship with the <u>Washington Monthly</u>. I appreciate the confidence that you obviously have in me and promise that I will not disappoint you. I am sure my work with you will help me with my journalism studies when I return to school in the fall.

I will plan to begin work on June 21, as we discussed. Please let me know if there is any paperwork I need to complete before reporting to work that day.

Sincerely,

Tracy Nelson

Tracy Nelson
<u>nelsont@aol.com</u>

Accepting Job Offer

7694 James Court
San Francisco, CA 94826

June 7, 20____

Judith Greene
Vice President
WEST COAST AIRLINES
2400 Van Ness
San Francisco, CA 94829

Dear Ms. Greene:

I am pleased to accept your offer, and I am looking forward to joining you and your staff next month.

The customer relations position is ideally suited to my background and interests. I assure you I will give you my best effort in making this an effective position within your company.

I understand I will begin work on July 1. If, in the meantime, I need to complete any paperwork or take care of any other matters, please contact me at 222-377-4029.

I enjoyed meeting with you and your staff and appreciated the professional manner in which the hiring was conducted.

Sincerely,

Joan Kitner

Joan Kitner
kitnerj@ace.net

Responding to Rejection

781 Humphrey Blvd.
Minneapolis, MN 53821

August 22, 20____

Sandra Delray
OLLEN GRAPHICS
182 Thompson Ave.
Suite 914
Minneapolis, MN 53824

Dear Ms. Delray:

I have just received your letter indicating that another candidate was selected for the position I interviewed for – a graphic artist. Of course I am disappointed, but I am sure you will be pleased with the person you selected.

I wish to take this opportunity to thank you for your consideration. I really appreciated the professional way in which the hiring process was conducted. I enjoyed meeting many of the artists in your firm and believe I would have worked well with them.

Please keep me in mind when you have another opening in your firm. I remain very interested in your company and the fine work you do.

Sincerely,

Debra Summers

Debra Summers
summersdeb@planet2.com

Responding to Rejection

179 W. 27th Street
San Francisco, CA 94131
October 3, 20____

Betsy Kramer
AMERICAN SCHOOL BOARDS
    ASSOCIATION
2792 Hillcrest Dr.
San Francisco, CA 94123

Dear Ms. Kramer:

I received your letter today, indicating that you had made a hiring decision. I regret that I was not the individual selected for the position, but I appreciate your letting me know of your decision in such a timely manner. I also appreciate the professional manner in which all aspects of the hiring process were conducted.

Please keep my resume on file. In fact, I am enclosing an additional copy for you in the event that the one I submitted earlier will be filed with other applications for the position you have already filled. I really believe my skills would be useful to your association and I know I would enjoy working with your staff. I would appreciate hearing from you if you should have a similar opening in the near future.

Thank you again for your consideration.

Sincerely,

Julie Stroomer

Julie Stroomer
stroomer@erols.com

Terminating Employment

6336 Boulder Avenue
Denver, CO 80976

July 31, 20____

Gerald Mockitis
General Manager
DENVER SUN TIMES
80796 County Line Road
Denver, CO 80911

Dear Mr. Mockitis:

When I accepted my position three years ago, I discussed with you
my plans to return to graduate school within 3-5 years. I have decided
that this is the best time for me to make this move, and hence I will
be resigning my position effective September 1st.

I want to thank you for the opportunity to work for the Sun Times. I
have learned a great deal about personnel administration, and my
experiences here have helped me to better focus on my goals for
graduate school.

I will miss all my colleagues at the Sun Times and hope to be able to
keep in touch with you over the next year.

Sincerely,

Alfred Merrill

Alfred Merrill
alfredmerrill@ace.net

Terminating Employment

1099 Seventh Avenue
Akron, OH 44522

August 2, 20____

James T. Thomas
Chief Engineer
AKRON CONSTRUCTION COMPANY
1170 South Hills Highway
Akron, OH 44524

Dear Jim,

I am writing to inform you that I will be leaving Akron Construction Company on September 12 to accept another position.

As you know, I have developed an interest in architectural drafting which combines my drafting skills with my artistic interests. While I was vacationing in Houston recently, a relative approached me about an opening for someone with my background with a large architecture and engineering firm. I investigated the possibility and subsequently received an offer. After careful consideration, I decided to accept the offer and relocate to Houston. I will be working with Brown and Little Company.

I have thoroughly enjoyed working with you over the past two years, and deeply appreciate your fine supervision and support. You have taught me a great deal about drafting, and I want to thank you for providing me with the opportunity to work here. It has been a very positive experience for me both personally and professionally.

I wanted to give you more than the customary two weeks notice so you would have time to find my replacement. I made the decision to relocate yesterday and decided to inform you immediately.

Best wishes.

Sincerely,

John Albert

John Albert
albertj@aol.com

11

Special and Unusual
Letters That Often Work

MOST LETTERS PRESENTED in this book are conventional job
search letters aimed at audiences that expect to receive such
"normal" letters. Going beyond the typical conventional letters,
our examples present job seekers as enthusiastic, intelligent,
capable, likable, focused, action-oriented, and persistent people – key personal
and professional characteristics sought by employers in candidates as well as
important ingredients for career success.

The Unconventional

Our final set of letters goes beyond the conventional – they operate on the edge
of what is considered to be acceptable or unacceptable job search communication. Not expecting to receive such communication from job seekers, employers
react to unconventional letters in different ways. Impressed by the writers
creativity, entrepreneurism, and drive, many employers remember, interview,
and hire such candidates. Other employers are turned off by the aggressive and
sometimes silly nature of such communication. Whatever the reaction, for
better or for worse, these forms of communication do grab the attention of
letter recipients.

We caution you about writing unconventional job search letters. Being on
the edge, they elicit different responses from different audiences. If, for example, you are applying for an artistic or sales position, you may want to demonstrate your creativity or entrepreneurialism in your written communication.
For the graphic artist, this might take the form of a special graphic incorpo-

rated in a letter. For someone in the print media, this could involve a headlined newspaper article about the individual reporting a story or a press release announcing an exceptional performer. For the salesperson, the classic letter accompanying the shoe-in-the-box has worked for some individuals who literally demonstrate their entrepreneurial nature by approaching strangers in such an unconventional manner. Many employers may feel such an approach may translate into new sales and clients.

Your Audience

Be your own judge as to the appropriateness of such unconventional communication. Keep in mind your audience. If, for example, you are applying for a position in banking, law, government, or education, remember the hiring cultures of these occupations tend to be conservative. On the other hand, the unconventional job search letter, memo, telegram, or card may sufficiently impress an employer to call you for an interview.

Whatever you do, know that in a job search there is no guarantee that anything works for every situation. How you choose to communicate – both message and medium – will tell the potential employer about how you will work with them.

Press Release
(Broadcast)

AUTOMOTIVE/   **For Immediate Release**
WAREHOUSE NEWS   Tel. 919-738-2981

Innovative Warehouse Inventory System Reduces Labor Costs By 35%!

Yes, it's true. A newly installed inventory system reduced labor costs by 35% at J. L. Automotive Parts. Mark Timpson, an employee with over seven years experience in parts management, developed an innovative inventory system custom-designed to meet the growing demand for used antique car parts. *"It really wasn't as difficult as I thought,"* Mark explains. *"I worked with a fine team of professionals who really know the parts business. We put our heads together over a three-week period to create a new computerized system that reduced our labor costs by 35% within eight months."*

For his team efforts, Mark received the Employee of the Year award. He believes this system is easily adapted to other automotive parts businesses and warehouse operations. He's prepared to demonstrate this approach to parties interested in strengthening their warehouse management systems.

#   #   #

For further information, including a detailed resume, or for scheduling an interview or demonstration, contact:

Mark Timpson
1873 Tyson Road
San Diego, CA 98712
Tel. 919-738-2981
timpsonm@aol.com
www.marktimpson.com

Shoe-in-the-Box
(resume inserted in shoe)

ANGEL ROBERTS   robertsa@aol.com

819 Collier Drive   ■   San Jose, CA 94011   ■   917-371-9021

July 19, 20____

Milton Whitehead
Director of Sales
SATURN PHARMACEUTICAL CO.
7213 American Drive
St. Louis, MO 63811

Dear Mr. Whitehead:

Now that I have my shoe in the door, how about an interview?

Expecting a call,

Angel Roberts

Angel Roberts

Enclosures: Angel's right shoe with resume stuffed inside

Telegram or E-mail

RESUME ARRIVING TOMORROW NOON BY FEDERAL EXPRESS. PLEASE EXAMINE CAREFULLY. CANDIDATE (SHEILA WATSON) WITH THREE YEARS EXPERIENCE DEVELOPING HIGHLY SUC-CESSFUL ART LEASING PROGRAM WISHES TO INTERVIEW FOR RECENTLY ADVERTISED LEASING MANAGER POSITION. ENCLOSING SAMPLE BROCHURES AND STRATEGIC MARKET-ING PLAN FOR YOUR REVIEW. EXPECTING EXCELLENT MARKET IN SECOND HALF OF YEAR BASED ON RECENT ANALYSIS OF CORPORATE ART ACQUISITION PATTERNS. WILLING TO TRAVEL AND RELOCATE. CALL 317-378-9871, FAX 317-378-8712, OR EMAIL WATSONS@ACE.COM FOR MORE INFORMATION OR APPOINTMENT.

3 x 5 Announcement Card

Where can you find fresh talent for promoting renewable energy resource issues?

I may be just out of college, but I have something most other college graduates lack – three years of environmental activism at both the state and local levels. I love producing results that contribute to protecting the environment. By June of next year, I want to be your most effective lobbyist throughout California.

You'll find my resume on the back of this card. Let's talk soon. I think we could work well together on issues we both are committed to seeing translated into public policy.

CONTACT: Janet Trueblood
Tel. 216-332-3829
truebloodj@aol.com

12

Have You Done Your Very Best?

THE PREVIOUS CHAPTERS presented examples of 201 job search letters based on the writing principles outlined in Chapter 2. As we noted earlier, use our examples for tips in developing strategies and composing your own unique set of job search letters that follow these principles. You should never copy or edit such examples.

Evaluate Yourself

If you want to create your very best letters, we recommend initially subjecting each of your letters to two different types of evaluations. The first type of evaluation is an **internal evaluation**. This is a self-evaluation you conduct yourself by examining your actions in reference to specific performance criteria. This evaluation helps you better structure, organize, produce, distribute, and follow up your letters according to the principles in Chapter 2.

The second type of evaluation may be more important than the internal evaluation. This is an **external evaluation** which is conducted by someone other than yourself. You ask individuals whose judgment you respect to give you feedback on your job search actions. In the case of letters, you want to find two or three individuals who will read your letters and then give you frank feedback on your writing strengths and weaknesses. This external evaluation is the closest you will get to receiving realistic feedback from the actual letter recipient.

Internal Evaluation

Once you complete your first job search letter, conduct a thorough internal evaluation based upon the following criteria. Several of these criteria already appeared in previous chapters. They relate to each step in the letter writing process – structure, organization, production, distribution, and follow-up. Respond to each statement by circling the appropriate number to the right that most accurately describes your letter.

Criteria	Yes	Maybe	No
Audience			
1. I know the needs of my audience based upon my research of both the organization and the individual.	1	2	3
2. My letter clearly reflects an understanding of the needs of the organization and the letter recipient.	1	2	3
3. The letter recipient will remember me favorably based on the unique style and content of my letter.	1	2	3
4. My letter offers a benefit to the the reader.	1	2	3
Form, Structure, and Design			
5. Makes an immediate positive impression and is inviting to read.	1	2	3
6. First seven elements in letter (heading, date line, inside address, salutation, body, closing, signature lines) are present and adhere to the rules.	1	2	3
7. Body subdivided into 2-4 paragraphs.	1	2	3
8. Most paragraphs run no more than 5 lines.	1	2	3
9. Most sentences are 25 words or less in length.	1	2	3
10. Includes complete name and address of letter recipient.	1	2	3

11. Signed name strongly and confidently,
     using a fountain pen.   1   2   3

12. Selected a standard typing style.   1   2   3

13. Has a clean, crisp, uncluttered,
     and professional look.   1   2   3

14. Used a 1¼" to 1½" margin around
     the top, bottom, and sides.   1   2   3

15. Confined to a single page.   1   2   3

Organization and Content

16. Immediately grabs the reader's attention.   1   2   3

17. Presents most important ideas first.   1   2   3

18. Expressed concisely.   1   2   3

19. Relates to the reader's interests and needs.   1   2   3

20. Persuades the reader to take action.   1   2   3

21. Free of spelling, grammatical, and
     punctuation errors.   1   2   3

22. Incorporates the active voice.   1   2   3

23. Avoids negative words and tone; uses
     positive language throughout.   1   2   3

24. Expresses the "unique you."   1   2   3

25. Employer-centered rather than self-centered.   1   2   3

26. Stresses benefits the reader is likely to
     receive from the letter writer.   1   2   3

27. Demonstrates a clear purpose.   1   2   3

28. Sentences and paragraphs flow logically.   1   2   3

29. Includes complete contact information.   1   2   3

30. Expresses enthusiasm, energy, and fire.   1   2   3

31. Follows the ABC's (see page 16) of
    good writing.   1   2   3

Production Quality

32. Has an overall strong professional
    appearance sufficient to make an
    immediate favorable impression.   1   2   3

33. Used an inkjet or laser printer that
    produces sharp quality print.   1   2   3

34. Adjusted copy setting properly – not
    too dark, not too light.   1   2   3

35. Type appears neat, clean, and straight.   1   2   3

36. Printed with a standard type style
    and size.   1   2   3

37. Produced on a letter quality machine.   1   2   3

38. Proofread and ran "spellcheck" (if
    using a word-processing program) for
    possible spelling/typing errors.   1   2   3

39. Used good quality paper stock that both
    looks and feels professional.   1   2   3

40. Selected a paper color appropriate
    for my audience.   1   2   3

41. Compared to nine other business letters
    received over the past year, this is
    one of three best in appearance.   1   2   3

Distribution

42. Addressed to a specific name.   1   2   3

43. Used a No. 10 business or a 9" x 12"
    envelope.   1   2   3

44. Checked to make sure all enclosures
    got enclosed.   1   2   3

45. Matched the envelope paper stock and
    color to the stationery.   1   2   3

46.   Typed the address and return address.   1   2   3

47.   Affixed a commemorative stamp.   1   2   3

48.   Used a special delivery service for
      overnight delivery.   1   2   3

49.   Recorded delivery date in a letter log
      for future follow-up actions.   1   2   3

Follow-Up Actions

50.   Ended my letter with an action statement
      indicating I would contact the individual
      by phone within the next week.   1   2   3

51.   Filed copy of the letter in a daily
      follow-up file.   1   2   3

52.   Made the first follow-up call at the
      time and date indicated in my letter.   1   2   3

53.   Followed up with additional phone calls
      until I was able to speak directly with the
      person or received the requested information.   1   2   3

54.   Maintained a positive and professional
      attitude during each follow-up activity.
      Was pleasantly persistent and tactful
      during all follow-up calls. Never indicated
      I was irritated, insulted, or disappointed
      in not having my phone calls returned.   1   2   3

55.   Followed up the follow-up by sending a
      thank you letter genuinely expressing my
      appreciation for the person's time and
      information.   1   2   3

TOTAL   [   ]

Add the numbers you circled to the right of each statement to get a cumulative score. If your score is higher than 60, you need to work on improving your letters. Go back and institute the necessary changes to create a dynamite letter.

External Evaluation

You can best conduct an external evaluation of your letters by circulating them to two or more individuals. Choose people whose opinions are objective, frank, and thoughtful. Do not select friends and relatives who usually flatter you with positive comments. Professional acquaintances or people you don't know personally but whom you admire may be good evaluators. An ideal evaluator has experience in hiring people in your area of job interest. In addition to sharing their experience with you, they may refer you to other individuals who would be interested in your qualifications. If you choose such individuals to critique both your letter and resume, ask them for their frank reaction – not what they would politely say to a candidate sending these materials. You want them to role-play with you –a potential interview candidate. Ask your evaluators:

- "How would you react to this letter if you received it from a candidate? Does it grab your attention and interest you enough to talk with me?"

- "If you were writing this letter, what changes would you make? Any additions, deletions, or modifications?"

You should receive good cooperation and advice by approaching people for this external evaluation. In addition, you will probably get valuable unsolicited advice on other job search matters, such as job leads, job market information, and employment strategies.

In contrast to the closed and deductive nature of the internal evaluation, the external evaluation should be open-ended and inductive. Let your reader give you as much information as possible on the quality and potential impact of your letter. Taken together, the internal and external evaluations should complement each other and provide you with maximum information.

Organize Your Campaign With Key Letters

In today's job market, the average job seeker takes between three and six months to find a new job. Let's assume the best: you offer excellent skills, are highly motivated, well organized, and willing to spend at least 20 hours a week on your job search. If this best characterizes your approach to the job search, we expect you will connect with a new job within three months.

The figure on page 261 summarizes the sequencing of a well organized job search campaign over a six-month period. During this time you should write numerous letters – a minimum of ten each week – as outlined in the previous chapters and identified for each step in Chapter 1 (page 4). Each letter will help you move closer to getting interviews and job offers – the ultimate goals of your letter writing activities. Use the forms on pages 262-267 to organize your letter writing campaign for each stage of your job search.

If after 12 weeks you are still looking for a job, review your job search activities. Evaluate how much time and effort you have put into high-impact job search activities. For example, have you written at least seven different types of letters? Have you written a minimum of ten such letters each week as documented in your letter writing plan/log on pages 262-267 (120 letters written thus far)? Do not count broadcast letters in your total since these letters are, by definition, relatively ineffective. What percentage of your letters have been approach and thank you letters?

If your answers to these questions are positive but you're not experiencing many successes (invitations to interview), then you should dramatically increase your letter writing activities. Rather than write a minimum of ten letters each week, consider increasing the number to 30 each week. At least 50 percent of your letters should be approach and thank you letters – the two most effective letters you should regularly write throughout your job search. Therefore, during the next 12 weeks you should write a minimum of 360 letters.

Organization of Job Search Activities

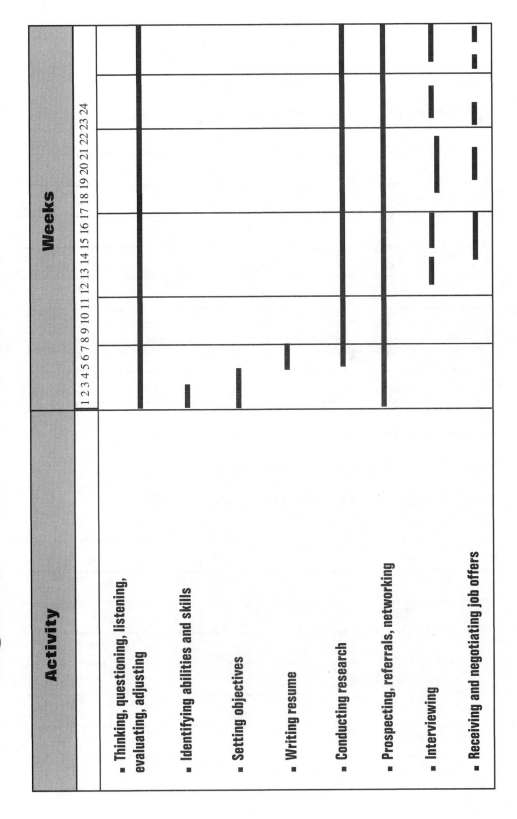

Activity	Weeks
	1 2 3 4 5 6 7 8 9 10 11 12 13 14 15 16 17 18 19 20 21 22 23 24
▪ Thinking, questioning, listening, evaluating, adjusting	
▪ Identifying abilities and skills	
▪ Setting objectives	
▪ Writing resume	
▪ Conducting research	
▪ Prospecting, referrals, networking	
▪ Interviewing	
▪ Receiving and negotiating job offers	

My Letter Writing Plan and Log
(Letters I must write)

WEEK 1: (number of letters I will write this week: _____)

Type of Letter   **Targeted Audience** (name/address)

_____   _____

_____   _____

_____   _____

_____   _____

_____   _____

_____   _____

_____   _____

_____   _____

_____   _____

WEEK 2: (number of letters I will write this week: _____)

Type of Letter   **Targeted Audience** (name/address)

_____   _____

_____   _____

_____   _____

_____   _____

_____   _____

_____   _____

_____   _____

WEEK 3: (number of letters I will write this week: _____)

Type of Letter   **Targeted Audience** (name/address)

_____   _____

_____   _____

_____   _____

_____   _____

_____   _____

_____   _____

_____   _____

_____   _____

_____   _____

_____   _____

WEEK 4: (number of letters I will write this week: _____)

Type of Letter   **Targeted Audience** (name/address)

_____   _____

_____   _____

_____   _____

_____   _____

_____   _____

_____   _____

_____   _____

_____   _____

_____   _____

_____   _____

WEEK 5: (number of letters I will write this week: _____)

Type of Letter   **Targeted Audience** (name/address)

_____   _____

_____   _____

_____   _____

_____   _____

_____   _____

_____   _____

_____   _____

_____   _____

_____   _____

_____   _____

WEEK 6: (number of letters I will write this week: _____)

Type of Letter   **Targeted Audience** (name/address)

_____   _____

_____   _____

_____   _____

_____   _____

_____   _____

_____   _____

_____   _____

_____   _____

_____   _____

_____   _____

WEEK 7: (number of letters I will write this week: _____)

Type of Letter   **Targeted Audience** (name/address)

_____   _____

_____   _____

_____   _____

_____   _____

_____   _____

_____   _____

_____   _____

_____   _____

_____   _____

_____   _____

WEEK 8: (number of letters I will write this week: _____)

Type of Letter   **Targeted Audience** (name/address)

_____   _____

_____   _____

_____   _____

_____   _____

_____   _____

_____   _____

_____   _____

_____   _____

_____   _____

_____   _____

WEEK 9: (number of letters I will write this week: _____)

Type of Letter   **Targeted Audience** (name/address)

_____   _____

_____   _____

_____   _____

_____   _____

_____   _____

_____   _____

_____   _____

_____   _____

_____   _____

_____   _____

WEEK 10: (number of letters I will write this week: _____)

Type of Letter   **Targeted Audience** (name/address)

_____   _____

_____   _____

_____   _____

_____   _____

_____   _____

_____   _____

_____   _____

_____   _____

_____   _____

_____   _____

WEEK 11: (number of letters I will write this week: _____)

Type of Letter   **Targeted Audience** (name/address)

_____   _____

_____   _____

_____   _____

_____   _____

_____   _____

_____   _____

_____   _____

_____   _____

_____   _____

_____   _____

WEEK 12: (number of letters I will write this week: _____)

Type of Letter   **Targeted Audience** (name/address)

_____   _____

_____   _____

_____   _____

_____   _____

_____   _____

_____   _____

_____   _____

_____   _____

_____   _____

_____   _____

The Authors

FOR MORE THAN TWO DECADES Ron and Caryl Krannich, Ph.Ds, have pursued a passion – assisting hundreds of thousands of individuals, from students, the unemployed, and ex-offenders to military personnel, international job seekers, and CEOs, in making critical job and career transitions. Focusing on key job search skills, career changes, and employment fields, their impressive body of work has helped shape career thinking and behavior both in the United States and abroad. Their sound advice has changed numerous lives, including their own!

Ron and Caryl are two of America's leading career and travel writers who have authored, co-authored, or ghost-written more than 70 books. A former Peace Corps Volunteer and Fulbright Scholar, Ron received his Ph.D. in Political Science from Northern Illinois University. Caryl received her Ph.D. in Speech Communication from Penn State University. Together they operate Development Concepts Incorporated, a training, consulting, and publishing firm in Virginia.

The Krannichs are both former university professors, high school teachers, management trainers, and consultants. As trainers and consultants, they have completed numerous projects on management, career development, local government, population planning, and rural development in the United States and abroad. Their career books focus on key job search skills, military and civilian career transitions, government and international careers, travel jobs, and nonprofit organizations and include such classics as *High Impact Resumes and Letters*, *Interview for Success*, and *Change Your Job, Change Your Life*. Their books represent one of today's most comprehensive collections of career writing. With nearly 3 million copies in print, their publications are widely available in bookstores, libraries, and career centers. No strangers to the Internet world, they have written *America's Top Internet Job Sites* and *The Directory of Websites for International Jobs* and published several Internet recruitment and job search books. They also have developed career-related websites: impactpublications.com, winningthejob.com, contentforcareers.com, and veteransworld.com. Many of their career tips have appeared on such major websites as monster.com, careerbuilder.com, employmentguide.com, and campuscareercenter.com.

Ron and Caryl live a double life with travel being their best kept *"do what you love"* career secret. Authors of over 20 travel-shopping guidebooks on various destinations around the world, they continue to pursue their international and travel interests through their innovative ***Treasures and Pleasures of . . . Best of the Best*** travel-shopping series and related websites: ishop aroundtheworld.com, contentfortravel.com, and travel-smarter.com. When not found at their home and business in Virginia, they are probably somewhere in Europe, Asia, Africa, the Middle East, the South Pacific, the Caribbean, or Latin Americas following their other passion – researching and writing about quality antiques, arts, crafts, jewelry, hotels, and restaurants as well as adhering to the career advice they give to others: *"Pursue a passion that enables you to do what you really love to do."*

As both career and travel experts, the Krannichs' work is frequently featured in major newspapers, magazines, and newsletters as well as on radio, television, and the Internet. Available for interviews, consultation, and presentations, they can be contacted as follows:

Ron and Caryl Krannich

krannich@impactpublications.com

Career Resources

THE FOLLOWING CAREER RESOURCES are available directly from Impact Publications. Full descriptions of each title, as well as 10+ downloadable catalogs and 40+ specialty flyers, can be found on Impact's website: www.impactpublications.com. Complete the following form or list the titles, include shipping (see formula at the end), enclose payment, and send your order to:

IMPACT PUBLICATIONS
9104 Manassas Drive, Suite N
Manassas Park, VA 20111-5211 USA
1-800-361-1055 (orders only)
Tel. 703-361-7300 or Fax 703-335-9486
E-mail address: info@impactpublications.com
Quick & easy online ordering: www.impactpublications.com

Orders from individuals must be prepaid by check, money order, or major credit card. We accept telephone, fax, and e-mail orders.

Qty.	TITLES	Price	TOTAL
____	5 Patterns of Extraordinary Careers	$17.95	____
____	95 Mistakes Job Seekers Make & How to Avoid Them	$13.95	____
____	101 Secrets of Highly Effective Speakers	$15.95	____
____	201 Dynamite Job Search Letters	$19.95	____
____	The $100,000+ Job Interview	$19.95	____
____	America's Top 100 Jobs for People Without a Four-Year Degree	$19.95	____
____	America's Top Internet Job Sites	$19.95	____
____	Best Cover Letters for $100,000+ Jobs	$24.95	____
____	Best Resumes for $100,000+ Jobs	$24.95	____
____	Best KeyWords for Resumes, Cover Letters, & Interviews	$17.95	____
____	Change Your Job, Change Your Life	$21.95	____
____	Discover the Best Jobs for You	$15.95	____
____	Dressing Smart for Men	$16.95	____
____	Dressing Smart for Women	$16.95	____
____	Dynamite Salary Negotiations	$15.95	____
____	Get a Raise in 7 Days	$14.95	____
____	Haldane's Best Answers to Tough Interview Questions	$15.95	____
____	Haldane's Best Cover Letters for Professionals	$15.95	____
____	Haldane's Best Resumes for Professionals	$15.95	____

270

____	High Impact Resumes and Letters	$19.95 _____
____	I Want to Do Something Else, But I'm Not Sure What It Is	$15.95 _____
____	KeyWords to Nail Your Job Interview	$17.95 _____
____	Interview for Success	$15.95 _____
____	The Job Hunting Guide: Transitioning From College to Career	$14.95 _____
____	Job Interview Tips for People With a Not-So-Hot Background	$14.95 _____
____	Military Resumes and Cover Letters	$21.95 _____
____	Nail the Job Interview	$13.95 _____
____	No One Will Hire Me!	$13.95 _____
____	Now, Discover Your Strengths	$27.00 _____
____	Occupational Outlook Handbook	$16.90 _____
____	Quit Your Job and Grow Some Hair	$15.95 _____
____	Rites of Passage at $100,000 to $1 Million+	$29.95 _____
____	Salary Negotiation Tips for Professionals	$16.95 _____
____	Savvy Interviewing: The Nonverbal Advantage	$12.95 _____
____	The Savvy Networker	$13.95 _____
____	Seven Habits of Highly Effective People	$15.00 _____
____	What Color Is Your Parachute?	$17.95 _____
____	What Should I Do With My Life?	$14.95 _____

SUBTOTAL _____

Virginia residents add 5% sales tax _____

POSTAGE/HANDLING ($5 for first
product and 8% of SUBTOTAL) $5.00

8% of SUBTOTAL --- _____

TOTAL ENCLOSED ----------------------------------- _____

SHIP TO:

NAME _____

ADDRESS: _____

_____

_____

PAYMENT METHOD:

❑ I enclose check/money order for $ _____ made payable to IMPACT PUBLICATIONS.

❑ Please charge $ _____ to my credit card:

❑ Visa   ❑ MasterCard   ❑ American Express   ❑ Discover

Card # _____ Expiration date: ____/____

Signature _____

Keep in Touch . . .
On the Web!

www.impactpublications.com
www.ishoparoundtheworld.com
www.travel-smarter.com
www.contentfortravel.com
www.winningthejob.com
www.veteransworld.com
www.contentforcareers.com